Fact File 2016

Statistics brought alive

All the facts and statistics you need to understand our world.
In print in this book & online as part of
Complete Issues

Complete Issues
articles · statistics · contacts

Complete Issues
articles · statistics · contacts

www.completeissues.co.uk

Your log in details:

Username: _____

Password: _____

Fact File 2016

The statistics behind the issues and controversies

Fact File 2016 is part of **Complete Issues**, a unique combination of resources online and in print.

Using **www.completeissues.co.uk** you can view individual pages from this book on screen, download, print, use on whiteboards and adapt to suit your needs. It makes Fact File even more flexible and useful.

In addition to the online service, you have this attractive printed version always available. Its clear presentation encourages users to feel confident about using and understanding statistical information and to browse and enjoy the data.

Because you have both the book and online access you can use Fact File in different ways with different groups and in different locations. It can be used simultaneously in the library, in the classroom and at home.

You can search for statistics secure in the knowledge that you will find meaningful data from reliable sources.

Your purchase of the book gives you access to Fact File PDFs via Complete Issues on one computer at a time. You can find your access codes on your covering letter or by contacting us. It is useful to record them on page 1 of this volume.

You can upgrade your online Fact File access with the **Online Expansion Pack**. This includes an unlimited site licence to make the service and the material available to all students and staff at all times, even from home. It also unlocks additional features such as interactive graphs and the search facility. You can find details here: www.carelpress.co.uk/factfile

Upgrading to a full **Complete Issues** subscription expands your resources further with combined access to articles, statistics and contacts. In addition, you gain access to our Focus Guides on specific topics - special selections giving you a quick and easy research focus on vital issues.

Complete Issues

Complete Issues gives you the statistics, articles and contacts to understand the world we live in. The unique format means that this information is available on the shelf and on the screen.

Complete Issues has been redesigned this year to make it even more user-friendly.

How does Complete Issues work?

All the pages are available to view online and download as PDFs and there are references and links to other parts of Complete Issues - the archive of articles, the statistics and the website and contact details of relevant organisations.

The statistics in Fact File, the articles in the Essential Articles series and online contacts work beautifully together on the Complete Issues website to produce a choice of relevant data, opinion and links.

When you search for a topic you instantly generate a list of relevant articles, figures and organisations with a thumbnail of the page and a short description.

The **advantages of Complete Issues** over just googling are:

- varied & reliable sources
- moderated - so appropriate for student use
- properly referenced
- beautifully presented
- ideal for classroom use
- cleared for copyright
- links that are checked for safety and relevance

The **Focus Guides** offer a selection from Complete Issues as a starting point for quick and easy access to information on important topics.

New material is added throughout the year and we will alert you to this and when issues become particularly topical

If you do not yet have the other resources in Complete Issues - the articles and the contacts - you can sample the service and upgrade here:

www.completeissues.co.uk

Complete Issues

articles · statistics · contacts

Published by Carel Press Ltd
4 Hewson St, Carlisle CA2 5AU
Tel +44 (0)1228 538928, Fax 591816
office@carelpress.co.uk
www.carelpress.com
© Carel Press

Research, design and editorial team:
Anne Louise Kershaw, Debbie Maxwell, Christine A Shepherd, Chas White, Thomas Mault

Subscriptions: Ann Batey (Manager), Brenda Hughes

British Library Cataloguing in Publication Data
A catalogue record for this book is available from the British Library

ISBN 978-1-905600-49-6

Printed by Finemark, Poland

FACT FILE 2016 CONTENTS

"My parents don't allow me to do anything else apart from revision and if I try and talk to them it always ends up in an argument."

page 30

"It's amazing what a stranger has done for me by donating their kidney. I can't thank them enough."

page 110

"...when hopelessness sets in, many will cross borders and become refugees."

page 147

Britain &
its citizens

Telling the truth

Who do we think are the most trustworthy people?

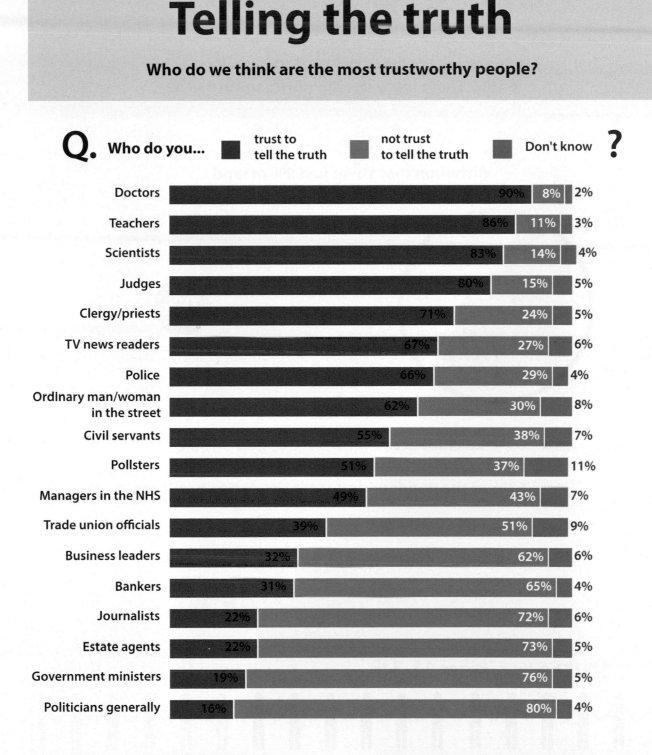

Q. Who do you... | ■ trust to tell the truth | ■ not trust to tell the truth | ■ Don't know **?**

	trust	not trust	don't know
Doctors	90%	8%	2%
Teachers	86%	11%	3%
Scientists	83%	14%	4%
Judges	80%	15%	5%
Clergy/priests	71%	24%	5%
TV news readers	67%	27%	6%
Police	66%	29%	4%
Ordinary man/woman in the street	62%	30%	8%
Civil servants	55%	38%	7%
Pollsters	51%	37%	11%
Managers in the NHS	49%	43%	7%
Trade union officials	39%	51%	9%
Business leaders	32%	62%	6%
Bankers	31%	65%	4%
Journalists	22%	72%	6%
Estate agents	22%	73%	5%
Government ministers	19%	76%	5%
Politicians generally	16%	80%	4%

Base 1,166 GB adults aged 15+
NB Figures may not add up to 100% due to rounding

Some issues

- Does this list match with the type of people you think are most trustworthy?

- Can you think of a reason why the groups who score highly would be the most trusted?

- Do the groups who score lowest have anything in common?

- What sort of things might change the levels of trust from one time to another?

Source: Trust in professions - Ipsos MORI, 2015   www.ipsos-mori.com

Cities

Cities are vital to life in the UK, but not all cities are equal. There is a widening north/south divide

Although they cover just 9% of land ...

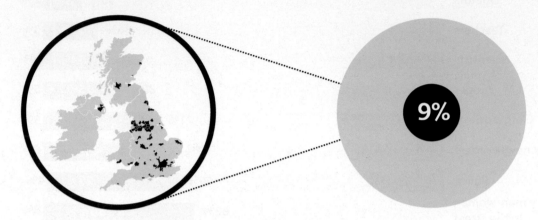

9%

**.... cities account for 54 % of population,
almost 60% of jobs and
63% of the goods and services the nation produces**

Population growth

Southern cities: 11.3%   **Other UK cities 5.5%**

The UK's four biggest cities - London, Birmingham, Manchester and Glasgow – account for **23.6%** of the UK's population. London alone is home to **15%.**

Between 2004 and 2013, cities in the South grew at **double** the rate of cities elsewhere.

8 of the 10 cities with the highest population growth are in the south.

All 10 of the cities with the lowest population growth are in the north of the UK.

Business growth

Southern cities: 26.8%

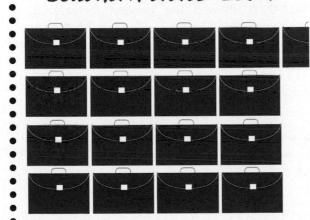

Other UK cities: 13.7%

The number of businesses in a city and the rate at which businesses are starting or closing tell us about the health of that city's economy. Cities in the South saw a much larger increase in the number of businesses between 2004 and 2013.

However, the individual cities with the largest growth were spread across the country - for example Aberdeen and Warrington saw some of the largest increases.

Only two cities ended the period with fewer businesses. **Blackpool** lost 550 businesses - a **fall** of **5.3%** and **Grimsby** lost 245, a **fall** of **5.5%**.

Job growth and earnings

Southern cities: 12.4%

Other UK cities: 0.9%

The biggest north/south divide shows up in the number of jobs created. The growth in the south was far greater than everywhere else, so much so that for every **12 jobs added** in the south, **only one** was added in the rest of Britain.

Seven of the top 10 cities for employment are **within 80 miles of London**.

At the other end of the scale, **six out of the 10 bottom cities** are concentrated in the North West and Yorkshire regions.

In 2014, the average weekly earnings in cities were **£538**, compared with the UK average of **£501**.

Workers in 14 cities earned above the national average but only four of these (Aberdeen, Derby, Edinburgh and Coventry) are located outside the Greater South East.

The gap between the top city and the bottom city widened so on average workers in **London** now earn on average **£282 more** per week than workers in **Huddersfield**.

Housing growth and costs

Southern cities:
housing growth - 470,000
population growth - 1.6m

Other UK cities:
housing growth - 430,000
population growth - 1m

Greater growth in business and work opportunities and therefore greater population growth meant that demand for new housing rose more in cities in the South than other cities. Although more houses were built in the South, the rising population meant that the demand was greater which in turn increased costs. By 2014, houses in cities in the South had become even more expensive than before.

Southern cities: 13.2 times earnings

Other UK cities: 6.7 times earnings

It is possible to measure affordable housing by comparing average prices to average wages.

In 2004 the average house in a city in the South cost **nine times** average earnings. By 2014 it had grown to more than **13 times** the average wage. There was virtually no change in cities elsewhere.

London showed the greatest increase. By 2014 the average house cost almost **16 times** average earnings, up from **9.5** in 2004.

Unequal neighbours

Inequalities **within** cities are often starker than **between** cities. There are often large differences between neighbourhoods. One way to measure this is to look at areas with a large percentage of benefit claimants and others with almost no claimants.

On this measure, **Aldershot** is the most equal city and **Belfast** is the least equal.

Some issues

- Does it matter that some cities are more prosperous than others?

- How could a city in decline change things?

- Could the national government make sure that prosperity is spread more equally?

- What features make up a great city to live in?

Source: Cities Outlook 2015 www.centreforcities.org

Neighbours

Strong neighbourhoods are still an essential part of life in Great Britain... but people tend to hold back from connecting with each other

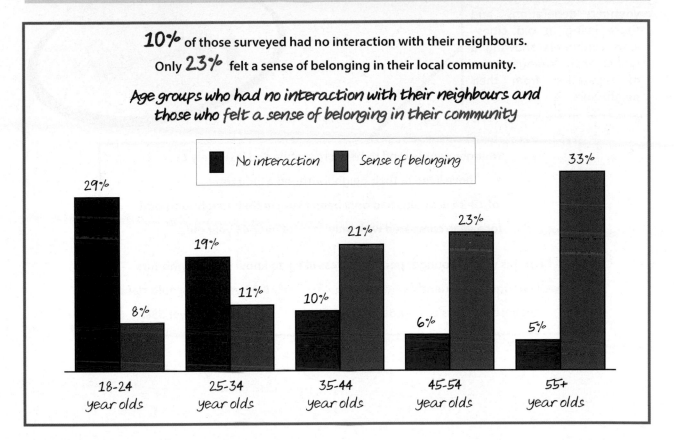

10% of those surveyed had no interaction with their neighbours.

Only **23%** felt a sense of belonging in their local community.

Age groups who had no interaction with their neighbours and those who felt a sense of belonging in their community

Legend:
- ■ No interaction
- ■ Sense of belonging

	18-24 year olds	25-34 year olds	35-44 year olds	45-54 year olds	55+ year olds
No interaction	29%	19%	10%	6%	5%
Sense of belonging	8%	11%	21%	23%	33%

Just saying hello can help create a closer and friendlier neighbourhood

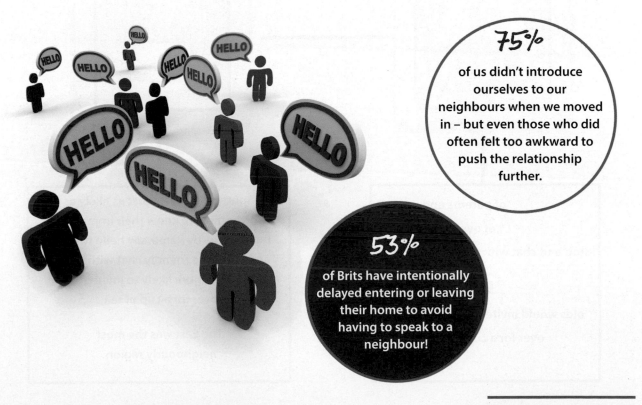

75% of us didn't introduce ourselves to our neighbours when we moved in – but even those who did often felt too awkward to push the relationship further.

53% of Brits have intentionally delayed entering or leaving their home to avoid having to speak to a neighbour!

We now tend to move further away from the neighbourhoods we grew up in. This has caused a long-term decline in communities coming together.

This is most noticeable in the younger generations and those living in big cities– with Londoners showing a higher than average sense of separation from their neighbours.

Younger people tend to be more mobile and less likely to have lived in their neighbourhood a long time. **25%** of 18-24 year olds had only been living in their neighbourhood for a year, compared with only **4%** of over-45 year olds.

For this reason younger people are less likely to know their neighbours well enough to be friends - **less than 20%** of 18-34 year olds would class their neighbours as friends compared to **almost 50%** of over 55s.

Britain's best chatters

57% of parents and **65%** of over 55s stop and chat with their neighbours.

Less than 25% of 18-34 year olds would invite their neighbours over for a cup of tea.

Southerners were just as likely as Northerners to know their immediate neighbours by name, say hello to them and stop for a friendly chat with them - and even more likely to invite them over for a cup of tea.

The East was the most neighbourly region.

Although almost **50%** of Brits would be comfortable leaving a key or contact number with neighbours when going on holiday, **20%** said they didn't have a single neighbour they would feel comfortable about asking to watch their home when on holiday. The most commonly mentioned reasons were not knowing them well enough or not wanting to bother them.

42% said they did not know their neighbours well enough

30% would not want to bother their neighbours

21% would not ask a neighbour to look after their property

22% did not trust their neighbours

16% would feel rude

25% would ask a neighbour to look after their property but not give them a key or an emergency contact

How to be a better neighbour

- Never just walk past, say hello.

- Offer a helping hand.

- Invite a neighbour over for a cup of tea, dinner, impromptu barbecue.

- Go online – join, or start, a forum or Facebook group for your neighbourhood, to share information on local facilities or as a safe platform to begin introductions and discussions.

- Help keep your neighbourhood tidy.

- Be considerate when parking your car.

- Offer to look out for a neighbour's property while they are on holiday. Swap house keys in case one of you gets locked out.

- Offer to take care of your neighbour's pets if they're going away.

- Receive parcels – if your neighbours aren't at home.

- Check on elderly neighbours.

Some issues

- Do you think it's important to have a good sense of community and relationship with your neighbours?

- Why do you think younger people are less close to their neighbours?

- Will young people have more sense of belonging as they grow older and settle?

- How useful is the advice in "How to be a better neighbour"?

Base: 2,340 GB adults aged 18+

Source: Knock-on Effect   www.comparethemarket.com

Home or abroad?

What do people miss when they move away from Britain?

Britishcornershop.co.uk is an online supermarket which delivers British food to those living abroad. It surveyed a cross section of its customers to find out what they missed most and least about Britain.

What they MISSED MOST about Britain
(top mentions)

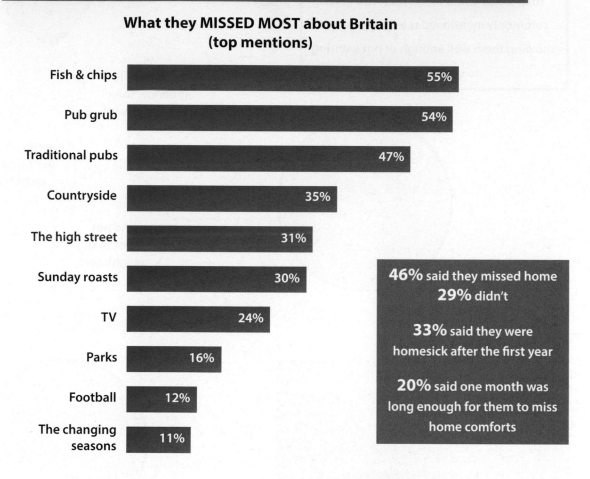

Fish & chips	55%
Pub grub	54%
Traditional pubs	47%
Countryside	35%
The high street	31%
Sunday roasts	30%
TV	24%
Parks	16%
Football	12%
The changing seasons	11%

46% said they missed home
29% didn't

33% said they were homesick after the first year

20% said one month was long enough for them to miss home comforts

What they MISSED LEAST about Britain
(top mentions)

Wet/cold weather	55%
Politicians	39%
Traffic	37%
Miserable people	34%
Commuting	26%
Sarcasm	13%
Annoying family members	10%
Bad neighbours	8%
Ex-partners	8%
The pound (£)	6%

Many people took more than a year to settle and feel comfortable in a new country while **10%** said they NEVER felt settled in their new location.

The hardest parts of settling abroad were missing family and friends **54%** and the language barrier **37%**.

Some issues

- What would you miss most if you went to live abroad?

- Why does food feature so strongly in the list?

- If you asked someone who had come to live in Britain the same questions, would their answers be similar?

- What would be the advantages of living in another country?

Base: 1,500 Britishcornershop.co.uk customers

Source: British Corner Shop www.Britishcornershop.co.uk

The survey showed that around **33%** of people had a worse impression of Britain than they did before they left.

Only **13%** said they thought better of the country.

Charity

TIME TO GIVE

Trust in charities

What does the public think of charities and the role they play in society?

Overall trust and confidence in charities

How much trust and confidence do you have in charities?
0 = don't trust them at all, 10= trust them completely

(Base: 1,163 adults aged 18+ in England and Wales)

| 0-4 | 5-7 | 8-10 | Don't know |

| 12% | 49% | 38% | 1% |

Average trust score 6.7

Those aged 18-34 had the highest level of trust with an average trust score of **7.0**, whilst people above retirement age gave charities a lower average score of **6.3**.

What is important to the public in terms of trust?

Most important aspects of trust and confidence in charities

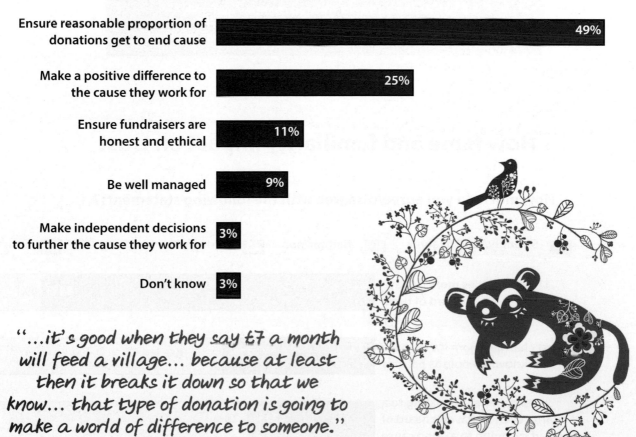

Ensure reasonable proportion of donations get to end cause	49%
Make a positive difference to the cause they work for	25%
Ensure fundraisers are honest and ethical	11%
Be well managed	9%
Make independent decisions to further the cause they work for	3%
Don't know	3%

"...it's good when they say £7 a month will feed a village... because at least then it breaks it down so that we know... that type of donation is going to make a world of difference to someone."

Male, London

The charities people trust

Reasons people give for trusting one charity or charity type more than others - top five mentions

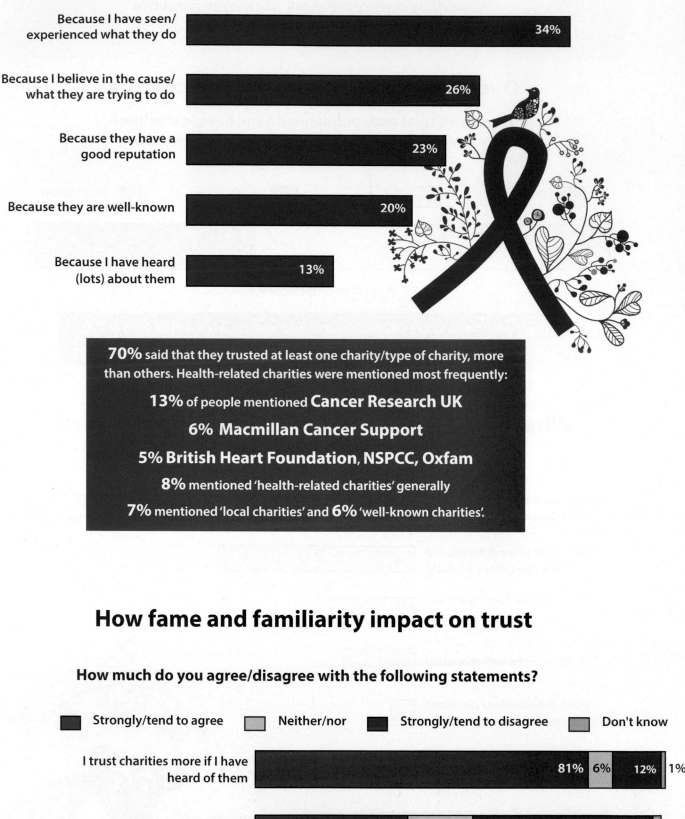

Because I have seen/ experienced what they do — 34%

Because I believe in the cause/ what they are trying to do — 26%

Because they have a good reputation — 23%

Because they are well-known — 20%

Because I have heard (lots) about them — 13%

70% said that they trusted at least one charity/type of charity, more than others. Health-related charities were mentioned most frequently:

13% of people mentioned **Cancer Research UK**

6% Macmillan Cancer Support

5% British Heart Foundation, NSPCC, Oxfam

8% mentioned 'health-related charities' generally

7% mentioned 'local charities' and **6%** 'well-known charities'.

How fame and familiarity impact on trust

How much do you agree/disagree with the following statements?

	Strongly/tend to agree	Neither/nor	Strongly/tend to disagree	Don't know

I trust charities more if I have heard of them — 81% | 6% | 12% | 1%

I trust charities more if they have well-known people as patrons — 37% | 16% | 44% | 2%

I feel confident donating to a charity even if I haven't heard of them, if it's going to a good cause — 31% | 10% | 58% | 2%

Which, if any of the following, are roles that you think charities should perform in society?

(Base: A survey of 1,035 GB adults aged 18+)

Helping communities (eg meals on wheels or helplines)	**56%**	Lobbying government to change law or policy	**32%**
Raising money for good causes	**51%**	Running a service that is currently run by the state (eg a library or probation service)	**11%**
Raising awareness of important issues in society	**47%**		
Encouraging people to volunteer	**44%**	None of these	**1%**
		Don't know	**2%**

Which, if any, of the following, do you think are the main things that charities are doing wrong?

(Three answers could be chosen)

Charities spend too much money on executive (senior management) salaries — 42%

Charities are not transparent about how they spend their money — 36%

Charities spend too much money abroad/ should focus on issues closer to home — 29%

Charities put too much pressure on people to donate — 29%

Charities spend too much money on running costs (including admin & marketing) — 26%

Charities are delivering public services that should be delivered by the state — 23%

Charities behave like a profit-making business — 15%

You never see the benefits of your donation — 14%

Charities spend too much money on employee salaries — 11%

Charities are not professional enough — 5%

I don't think charities make a difference/ I don't know what they achieve for their beneficiaries — 4%

Charities receive tax breaks which they aren't entitled to — 4%

None of these — 3%

Don't know — 2%

"I can't understand why they're sending money to all these different things when they're in trouble over here."

Female, London

Some issues

- Which charities would you support?

- Do you agree that sometimes charities put too much pressure on people?

- Should the government really provide the services that charities provide?

- Should senior managers who work for a charity be paid the same rate as senior managers who work in other industries, or should they take less?

Source: Ipsos MORI for Charity Commission - Public trust and confidence in charities & Ipsos MORI for New Philanthropy Capital - State of the Sector Survey www.ipsos-mori.com

The value of charity

A majority of British households use the services of charities - sometimes without realising it

There are over 161,000 charities in the UK

Many of us have had contact with them as donors, service users or volunteers.

2,070 adults were asked about their household's use of a wide range of charitable organisations or services covering six main areas:

- advice;
- direct support;
- community involvement;
- housing;
- education;
- retail.

Have you or other members of your household used any of these types of services in the last 12 months?

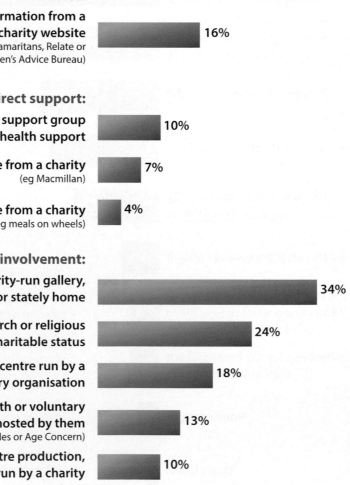

Advice:

Advice or information from a charity or from a charity website
(eg The Samaritans, Relate or The Citizen's Advice Bureau) — 16%

Direct support:

Attended counselling, support group or received mental health support — 10%

Medical care from a charity
(eg Macmillan) — 7%

Ongoing support/care from a charity
(eg meals on wheels) — 4%

Community involvement:

Visited a charity-run gallery, museum, garden or stately home — 34%

Visited a church or religious institution of charitable status — 24%

Visited a community centre run by a charity or voluntary organisation — 18%

Attended a community, youth or voluntary group or an event hosted by them
(eg the Scouts, Girl Guides or Age Concern) — 13%

Watched or participated in a theatre production, event or arts-related programme run by a charity — 10%

Have you or other members of your household used any of these types of services in the last 12 months?

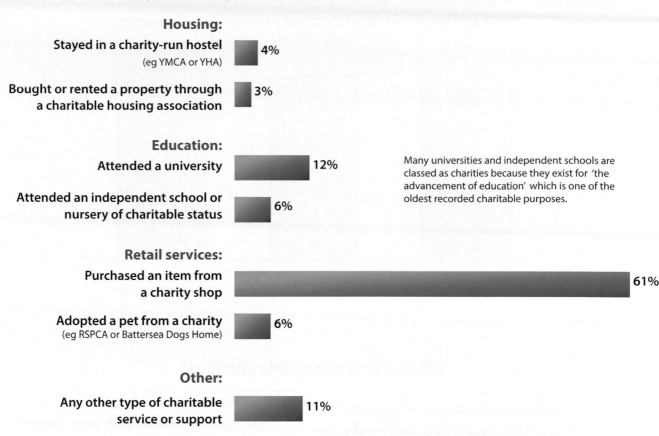

Housing:

Stayed in a charity-run hostel
(eg YMCA or YHA) — 4%

Bought or rented a property through a charitable housing association — 3%

Education:

Attended a university — 12%

Attended an independent school or nursery of charitable status — 6%

Many universities and independent schools are classed as charities because they exist for 'the advancement of education' which is one of the oldest recorded charitable purposes.

Retail services:

Purchased an item from a charity shop — 61%

Adopted a pet from a charity
(eg RSPCA or Battersea Dogs Home) — 6%

Other:

Any other type of charitable service or support — 11%

"We support [charities] and rely on them, from buying items in charity shops to help the causes close to our hearts to seeking advice from charities on a whole range of issues.

Many of us don't even realise we're using a charity, but even a trip to a National Trust property or a visit to a museum can be thanks to the wonderful work of charities in the UK."

Deborah Fairclough, head of research at the Charities Aid Foundation

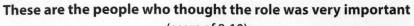

People were asked how important is the role that charities play in society?

Their scores could range between 1 - *not at all important* and 10 - *essential*

These are the people who thought the role was very important
(score of 8-10)

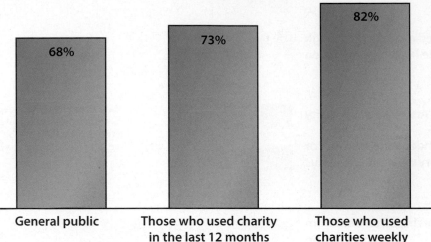

68%	73%	82%
General public	Those who used charity in the last 12 months	Those who used charities weekly

Who's using charitable services?

- **Women** were more likely to use charitable services: **83%** in the last 12 months, compared to **75%** of **men**.

- **85%** of those **aged 65 or over** said they'd used a charity service in the last 12 months, compared to only **75%** of those **aged 18–24**. However, younger people used a greater range of different charity services.

- **Families with older children** were most likely to have used a charitable service within the last 12 months - **89%**. Older couples and lone parents were the next biggest users - both **84%**.

- The households that were using charities the most ie families with older children, were most likely to see them as making a difference to their lives - **64%**.

- Older couples were much more likely than average to have bought an item in a charity shop - **72%** versus **61%** overall.

- Lone parents were more likely to have visited a community centre run by a charity or voluntary organisation - **33%** versus **18%** overall.

- **33%** of lone parents considered the charity services that they received as central to their lives, and said they would struggle without them.

- The middle classes use more charities than those on the lowest income:
  - Those earning over £55,000 are more likely to use a larger variety of charities than those with incomes of less than £14,000.

  - **Higher income earners** used **four** charities on average in the past year while those with **lower incomes** used less than **three**.

Personal benefits perceived by those who have used charities

Mentioned by % of respondents

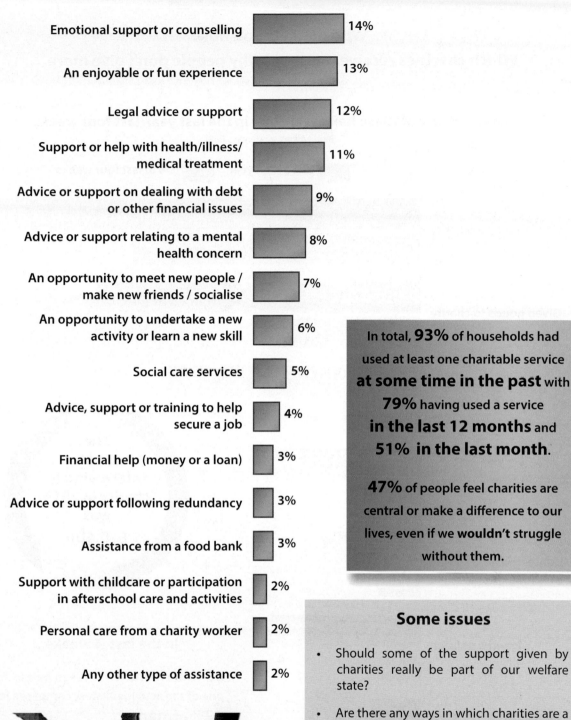

Emotional support or counselling	14%
An enjoyable or fun experience	13%
Legal advice or support	12%
Support or help with health/illness/ medical treatment	11%
Advice or support on dealing with debt or other financial issues	9%
Advice or support relating to a mental health concern	8%
An opportunity to meet new people / make new friends / socialise	7%
An opportunity to undertake a new activity or learn a new skill	6%
Social care services	5%
Advice, support or training to help secure a job	4%
Financial help (money or a loan)	3%
Advice or support following redundancy	3%
Assistance from a food bank	3%
Support with childcare or participation in afterschool care and activities	2%
Personal care from a charity worker	2%
Any other type of assistance	2%

In total, **93%** of households had used at least one charitable service **at some time in the past** with **79%** having used a service **in the last 12 months** and **51%** **in the last month**.

47% of people feel charities are central or make a difference to our lives, even if we **wouldn't** struggle without them.

Some issues

- Should some of the support given by charities really be part of our welfare state?

- Are there any ways in which charities are a better source of support than government agencies?

- The definition of a charity in this report ranges from organisations such as the RSPCA to independent schools such as Eton. Does this change the way you view some of the information?

- Can you suggest reasons why better off people appear to be using charities more than those on lower incomes?

Source: Charity Street: The value of charity to British households, Institute for Public Policy Research © IPPR 2014 www.ippr.org

UK giving

Who donates and how.
Which charities receive most and why people don't give more.

Which, if any of these have you done in the last year/last four weeks

(Base - All respondents: 5,068)

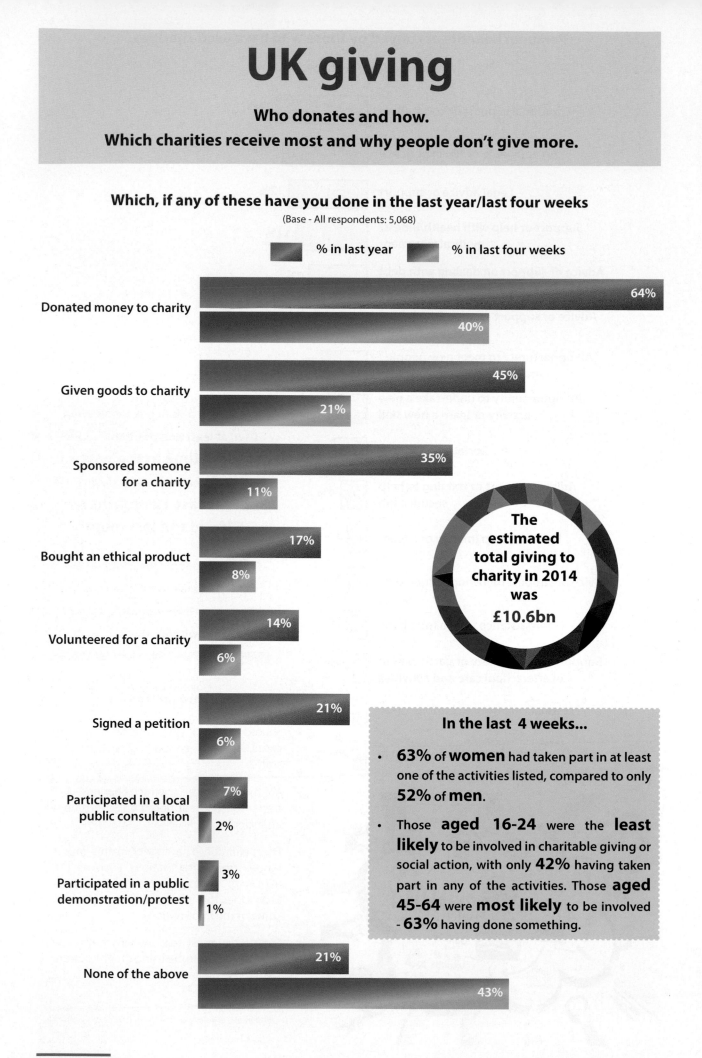

% in last year   % in last four weeks

Donated money to charity
- 64%
- 40%

Given goods to charity
- 45%
- 21%

Sponsored someone for a charity
- 35%
- 11%

Bought an ethical product
- 17%
- 8%

Volunteered for a charity
- 14%
- 6%

Signed a petition
- 21%
- 6%

Participated in a local public consultation
- 7%
- 2%

Participated in a public demonstration/protest
- 3%
- 1%

None of the above
- 21%
- 43%

The estimated total giving to charity in 2014 was £10.6bn

In the last 4 weeks...

- **63%** of **women** had taken part in at least one of the activities listed, compared to only **52%** of **men**.

- Those **aged 16-24** were the **least likely** to be involved in charitable giving or social action, with only **42%** having taken part in any of the activities. Those **aged 45-64** were **most likely** to be involved - **63%** having done something.

Proportion of donors giving to different causes

Base: all donating money in the last four weeks (2,252)

Proportion of total amount donated

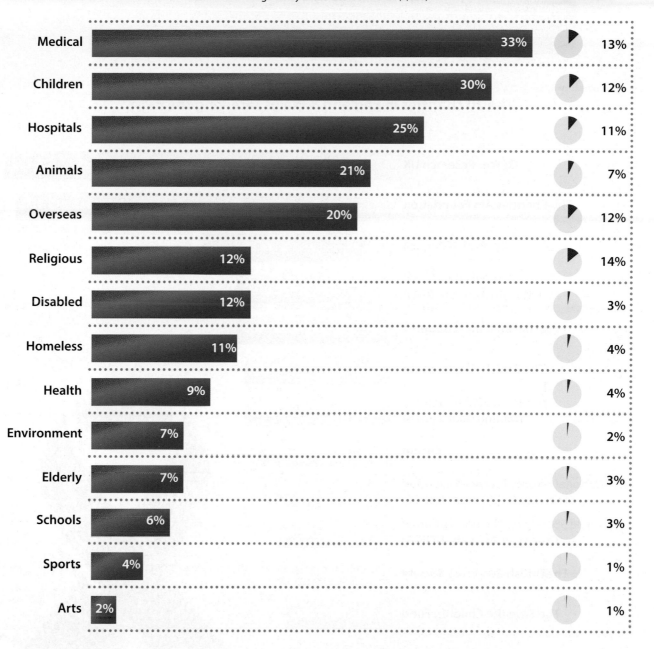

Cause	Proportion of donors giving	Proportion of total amount donated
Medical	33%	13%
Children	30%	12%
Hospitals	25%	11%
Animals	21%	7%
Overseas	20%	12%
Religious	12%	14%
Disabled	12%	3%
Homeless	11%	4%
Health	9%	4%
Environment	7%	2%
Elderly	7%	3%
Schools	6%	3%
Sports	4%	1%
Arts	2%	1%

Although they were supported by just **12%** of donors, **religious causes** received the largest proportion of the total amount donated. This was because the typical donation made to religious causes was **£20** - much higher than the average amount given which was **£14**.

The **Arts** received the next largest typical donation – **£12**.

Medical research and **hospitals** mostly received donations of **£8** and **children's causes** received **£10**.

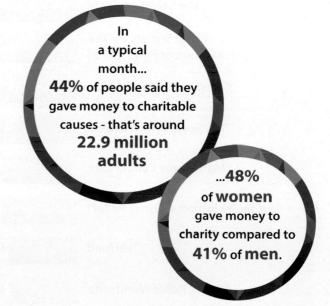

In a typical month...
44% of people said they gave money to charitable causes - that's around **22.9 million adults**

...**48%** of **women** gave money to charity compared to **41%** of **men**.

Voluntary income to charities is made up of different types of donations, for example: gifts and donations received (including legacies and endowments), any tax reclaimed on donations through Gift Aid, general grants and ones that provide the main financial funding, membership subscriptions and sponsorship where these are in effect donations, gifts in kind and donated services and facilities.

The 20 charities in England & Wales receiving the most voluntary income March 2015

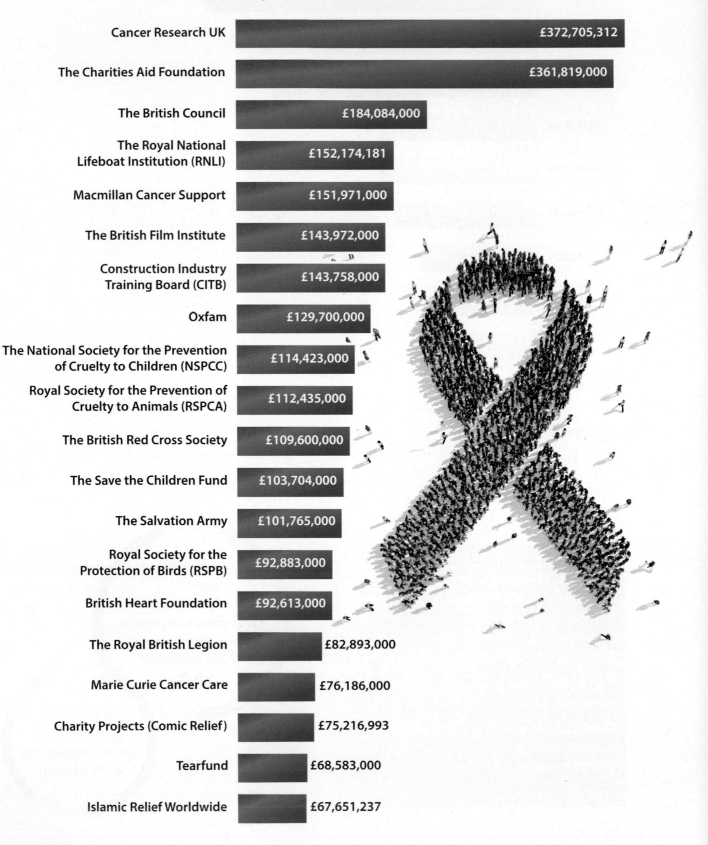

Charity	Voluntary income
Cancer Research UK	£372,705,312
The Charities Aid Foundation	£361,819,000
The British Council	£184,084,000
The Royal National Lifeboat Institution (RNLI)	£152,174,181
Macmillan Cancer Support	£151,971,000
The British Film Institute	£143,972,000
Construction Industry Training Board (CITB)	£143,758,000
Oxfam	£129,700,000
The National Society for the Prevention of Cruelty to Children (NSPCC)	£114,423,000
Royal Society for the Prevention of Cruelty to Animals (RSPCA)	£112,435,000
The British Red Cross Society	£109,600,000
The Save the Children Fund	£103,704,000
The Salvation Army	£101,765,000
Royal Society for the Protection of Birds (RSPB)	£92,883,000
British Heart Foundation	£92,613,000
The Royal British Legion	£82,893,000
Marie Curie Cancer Care	£76,186,000
Charity Projects (Comic Relief)	£75,216,993
Tearfund	£68,583,000
Islamic Relief Worldwide	£67,651,237

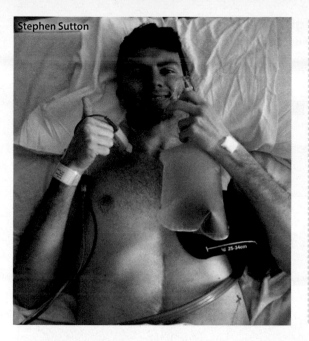
Stephen Sutton

Ways of giving

Cash was the most popular method of giving - used by **55%** of those donating money directly in the last year.

Social media campaigns in 2014 such as the #nomakeupselfie, Stephen Sutton's 'thumbs up' campaign, and the Ice Bucket Challenge helped to boost the use of **online** giving - used by **15%** of donors.

Giving by **text** was used by **11%** helped by larger fundraising events such as Comic Relief and Children in Need which use 'keyword' text donation methods.

Young donors

What 16-24 year olds did MORE of than donors overall:

*   'liked' a charitable organisation page via Facebook or similar: **23%** of 16-24 year olds compared to **13%** overall;

*   gave money via their mobile phones in the past year: **14%** compared to **8%** overall;

*   gave 'from time to time': **50%** compared to **44%** overall.

What they did LESS of than donors overall:

*   thought carefully about what charitable causes they donated money to: **61%** compared to **72%** overall;

*   supported the same charities every year: **37%** compared to **59%** overall.

Sponsorship

The typical monthly amount given by people who sponsored someone else was **£10.**

That is smaller than the overall average donation of **£16**. This may be because the donor was less interested in the cause and was just supporting the individual doing the activity.

People tend to pledge the same or a similar amount as other donors. This means it is likely that a large donation will be followed by others. But it could also mean lower donations if one individual makes a smaller than average donation.

Barriers to giving

Base: all UK Giving respondents, May 2014 (1,042)

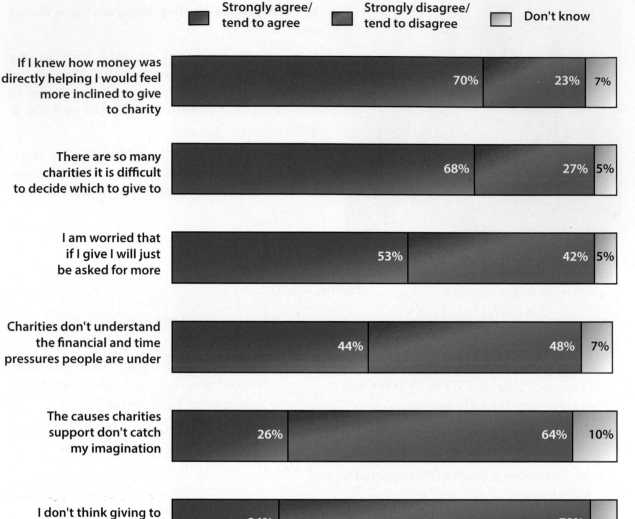

■ Strongly agree/ tend to agree ■ Strongly disagree/ tend to disagree ☐ Don't know

If I knew how money was directly helping I would feel more inclined to give to charity
70% | 23% | 7%

There are so many charities it is difficult to decide which to give to
68% | 27% | 5%

I am worried that if I give I will just be asked for more
53% | 42% | 5%

Charities don't understand the financial and time pressures people are under
44% | 48% | 7%

The causes charities support don't catch my imagination
26% | 64% | 10%

I don't think giving to charity makes a meaningful difference
24% | 70% | 6%

NB Figures may not add up to 100% due to rounding

Some issues

- Which causes would you give time or money to?

- Why were some internet campaigns so effective in raising money?

- Do you sympathise with any of the reasons for not giving?

- Why do you think different ages and genders contribute towards charity in different ways?

Source: UK Giving 2014 © Charities Aid Foundation 2015
www.cafonline.org

Education

School stress

Young people feel under pressure at school and many don't know where to turn for help

A survey of 2,000 young people aged 11-25 by YoungMinds revealed that a third didn't know where to turn to get help when they felt depressed or anxious.

When you have felt stressed or anxious at school, who did you talk to?

Your best friend	42.6%
Your classmates	16.2%
A teacher	15.6%
School counsellor	5.4%
Your tutor	6.5%
The school nurse	1.6%
Nobody	33.0%
Other	11.3%

I feel like a million things are going on in my head! ... I do not feel confident that I am going to get my predicted grades of A* and A but when I tell my teachers they just tell me not to worry and that I can do it.

Girl, 12-15 age group

Useful organisations

ChildLine: 0800 1111
www.childline.org.uk

YoungMinds: 020 7089 5050
Parent Helpline: 0808 802 5544
www.youngminds.org.uk

How much do you agree with the following statements?

I feel (or felt) like a failure if I don't (or didn't) get good grades

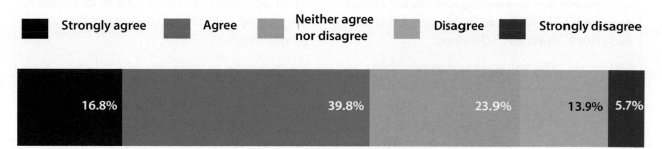

Strongly agree | **Agree** | **Neither agree nor disagree** | **Disagree** | **Strongly disagree**

| 16.8% | 39.8% | 23.9% | 13.9% | 5.7% |

I feel (or felt) as though my school is (or was) more worried about my grades than about me

| 16.8% | 32.1% | 29.6% | 16.8% | 4.7% |

The NSPCC's annual survey showed that in 2013/14 school and education problems such as exam pressures, concerns about performance, not coping with workload etc, appeared in the top ten concerns for the first time with **35,500** counselling sessions – a **13%** increase compared to 2012/13.

Age groups of those counselled for school and educational problems

16-18 (22%)

11 and under (16%)

12-15 (62%)

There was a 200% increase in counselling about exam stress

Where school and education was the main concern, 58% of counselling sessions were about exam stress. The NSPCC web page about this topic had **more than 87,500** views.

This stress affected young people's ability to sleep, triggered anxiety attacks, depression and tearfulness and eating disorders. In some cases it also led to self-harm and suicidal feelings.

School and education problems were mentioned as an additional concern in **10%** of self-harm counselling and **10%** of counselling with young people who felt suicidal.

Young people in lower sets worried about their peers seeing them as stupid. Those in the highest sets spoke about feeling under pressure to live up to other people's expectations.

All age groups worry about how exams will affect their future

The pressure of doing well was also linked to worries about what was coming up next for young people.

Children aged 11 and under were anxious about how their results would affect which secondary school they would go to and what group they would be placed in. Not doing well often raised doubts about being able to make new friends or provoked fears of being bullied.

I've got SATs coming up soon and I'm so worried! I'm going to the big school and it's a different one to where my friends are going.

Girl, 11 and under age group

There was a **30%** increase in school and education problems in the 16-18 age group due to young people feeling increased pressure and needing extra support in the run-up to and during their exams.

Photo posed by model

I think I'm going to fail my GCSEs and that makes me so worried for the future. What if I can't get a job anywhere?
I'm struggling in so many subjects and finding revision hard because I don't really know how to organise myself. I've been self-harming to deal with how scared I am.

Boy 12-15 age group

Achieving the right grades for university was a common worry for this age group. Many felt as if exams and results had become their 'whole life'.

Stresses around having to move out of home to attend college or university, being able to afford accommodation and managing bills were often mentioned.

My parents don't allow me to do anything else apart from revision and if I try and talk to them it always ends up in an argument.

Teenage boy who called ChildLine

I'm really feeling the pressure of A levels, I've been having panic attacks and difficulty breathing. I'm so afraid of not getting the right grades.

Boy, 16-18 age group

For those at university, the pressures of their course often made them want to leave but they felt that they had no choice but to keep going as they knew how disappointed their parents would be.

They also felt guilty about the money that their parents had already spent.

I am feeling very stressed and overwhelmed at the thought of going back to uni. I cannot cope with the pressure of my course and feel scared about going back as I have not done any revision for my exams.

Girl, 16-18 age group

Photo posed by model

Advice from ChildLine - how to cope with exams

- Take regular breaks from revising and do some exercise.

- Go to bed at a reasonable time and try to get some sleep.

- Try to think positively - even if you don't feel like it, a positive attitude will help you during your revision.

- Take some water into the test with you if you can - keeping hydrated by drinking water will help you concentrate.

Some issues

- Are the pressures on young people greater now than in the past?

- What could be done to help young people cope better?

- Is there an argument that stress is part of life and people should just learn to deal with it?

- If you had a problem who would you talk to?

Source: YoungMinds www.youngminds.org.uk
NSPCC ChildLine Review - Under pressure www.nspcc.org.uk

School uniform costs

The high cost of school uniforms is having an impact on many children's lives

1,007 parents of school age children across the UK were surveyed about the costs of school uniforms.

Overall, parents with children in state maintained schools said that they spent **£316 per year** on school uniform costs for **secondary** school children and **£251 per year** for **primary** school children.

95% of parents said the amount they paid was 'unreasonable'. Parents of **secondary** school children said they spent an average of **£188 per year more** than they thought 'reasonable' and for **primary** school children, **£151 per year more**.

This showed that, on average, parents overspent on school uniforms by **£170 per child each year.** Combined, all the parents could **save** as much as **£1.3 billion per year** if they faced reasonable school uniform costs.

Parents said that this was leading to children going to school in ill-fitting school uniform, being sent home from school or to families cutting back on food or other basic essentials.

Parents were asked:
How much on average do you pay for different items of school uniform?

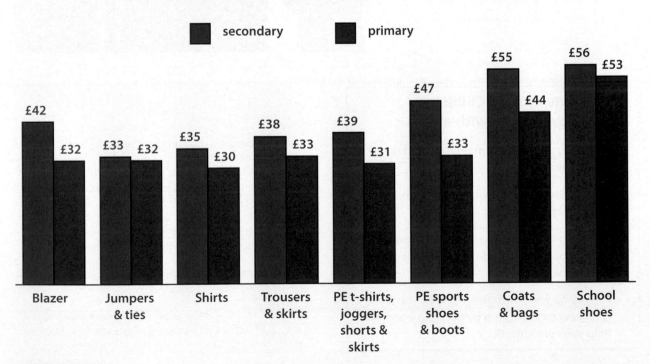

	secondary	primary
Blazer	£42	£32
Jumpers & ties	£33	£32
Shirts	£35	£30
Trousers & skirts	£38	£33
PE t-shirts, joggers, shorts & skirts	£39	£31
PE sports shoes & boots	£47	£33
Coats & bags	£55	£44
School shoes	£56	£53

One of the main reasons for the high costs are school uniform policies that make parents buy specific items of clothing and accessories from specialist shops, rather than allowing them to buy cheaper clothes from supermarkets and sew on a badge or logo later.

Where parents have to buy one or more items of school uniform from a specific supplier, costs were an average of **£48 per year higher** for **secondary** school children and **£93 higher** for **primary** school children.

Other reasons for high costs include schools requiring many different items of uniform including coats, different ties for different years in the school, and multiple items of sports kit.

What parents said were the effects of school uniform costs on their children's lives - Numbers of children affected

"I hate school because my mum and dad can't afford the trousers so I have to wear trackies. But my head of college...goes 'You've got to get your trousers sorted out!' "

Young person

220,000	480,000	330,000	780,000	1,160,000
Uniform costs affected the choice of school for their child	Their child wearing incorrect uniform	Their child wearing unclean uniform	Their child wearing ill-fitting uniform	One or more of these: incorrect, unclean or poorly fitting uniform

Photo posed by model

"My oldest daughter, they sent her home and said she wasn't allowed to come back until she had the correct shoes. So then I had to write a letter to say that we'll be able to get some in a week or so, I didn't have any money."

Parent

Some issues

- Does school uniform cause problems or solve them?

- Would not having a uniform cause any problems?

- What can schools do to make uniform policies fairer?

- If you were in charge of school uniform, what would you choose?

NB small base

Source: The Wrong Blazer, The Children's Commission on Poverty (CCP), Opinium Research survey
www.childrenscommission.org.uk

Value of university

Many students said their education was not value for money, but very few said they would NOT to go to university at all if they had the chance

As university grants were cut, students became almost fully responsible for the costs of their higher education.

The 1,004 final year undergraduate students surveyed were the first to pay higher fees of up to £9,000 per year, after the price of university tuition trebled in 2012.

Which of the following comes closest to your opinion about your university education?

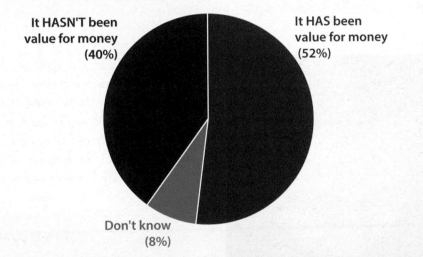

It HASN'T been value for money (40%)

It HAS been value for money (52%)

Don't know (8%)

The survey found there were differences of opinion between students doing different types of courses.

Average teaching time is just **under 12 hours** a week.

In arts courses, teaching time can be as little as **8 hours** a week, as there is much more emphasis on independent study.

But science courses, where students expressed a greater degree of satisfaction, tend to have more teaching time as well as access to laboratories and specialist equipment.

65% of those studying science, technology, maths and engineering - subjects that require a lot of practical teaching and staff time - said their courses had been good value.

And **44%** of humanities and social science students, which tend to receive less direct teaching time, said they felt their courses represented good value.

If you could start university again, which of the following do you think you would do?

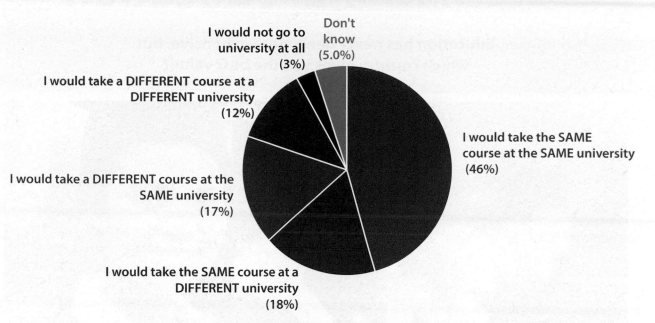

I would not go to university at all (3%)

Don't know (5.0%)

I would take a DIFFERENT course at a DIFFERENT university (12%)

I would take the SAME course at the SAME university (46%)

I would take a DIFFERENT course at the SAME university (17%)

I would take the SAME course at a DIFFERENT university (18%)

To what extent do you feel that university has prepared you for the future?

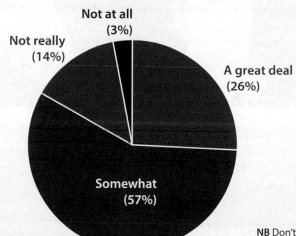

Not at all (3%)

Not really (14%)

A great deal (26%)

Somewhat (57%)

NB Don't knows amounted to less than 1%

Figures may not add up to 100% due to rounding

Some issues

- What do you think 'value for money' means in terms of education?

- If only 46% of all students feel that they have chosen the right course and the right university, does that mean there is something wrong with the process?

- Only a quarter of all students feel that university has fully prepared them for the future. Is that a reasonable expectation?

- Is it fair that students have to pay for higher education?

Source: ComRes for BBC Radio 5 Live   www.comres.co.uk

International education

Education has never been more expensive, but which country gives you the best value?

A survey of over 4,500 parents in 15 countries, suggests that parents recognise the value of a good education, but too many are still financially underprepared.

Some **89%** of parents said that they wanted their children to go to university, but **51%** wished they had started saving earlier for their child's education.

74% of parents around the world would consider sending their child abroad for a better university education.

51% globally rank the USA in their top three for countries that provide the highest quality of education.

But parents who think that 'west is best' in terms of the quality of education must face the reality that the costs are high.

38% of parents rated the UK in their top three countries for educational quality, but the annual costs including university fees and living costs are in excess of USD35,000 per year.

"The key reasons to send children overseas are the acquisition of foreign languages, international experience, and independence. The majority of overseas education is privately funded by parents, but while the concept of a college fund is well established in the United States, it is still the exception elsewhere."

Thies Clemenz, Chief Executive Officer, HSBC Bank Armenia

The **USA** and **China** rate each other in their top 3 for the quality of education they provide.

73% of Chinese parents think the USA offers a high quality education. However, it may be more cost effective for parents in the USA to send their children to university in China, with an annual overall cost of less than **USD11,000** per year.

At **USD2,000** a year, **Australia** – a very popular destination for Asian students – is the most expensive option.

Education costs around the world

Country	University Fees per year (USD)	Cost of Living per year (USD)	Cost Total per year (USD)	Cost Rank	Quality of Education Rank	% who rank country in top 3 for Quality of Education
Australia	$24,081	$18,012	$42,093	1	3	25
Singapore	$18,937	$20,292	$39,229	2	6=	10
United States	$24,914	$11,651	$36,564	3	1	51
United Kingdom	$21,365	$13,680	$35,045	4	2	38
Hong Kong	$13,444	$18,696	$32,140	5	7	6
Canada	$16,746	$13,201	$29,947	6	4	20
France	$247	$16,530	$16,777	7	6=	10
Malaysia	$2,453	$10,488	$12,941	8	9	3
Indonesia	$4,378	$8,527	$12,905	9	11=	1
Brazil	$59	$12,569	$12,627	10	11=	1
Taiwan	$3,338	$8,573	$11,911	11	10	2
Turkey	$1,276	$10,089	$11,365	12	11=	1
China	$3,844	$6,886	$10,729	13	5	13
Mexico	$750	$8,710	$9,460	14	11=	1
India	$581	$5,062	$5,642	15	8	5

Some issues

- Is it right that parents have to save for a university education or should it be free?

- What should be done for families who cannot afford to send their children to university?

- Do you agree that an education abroad is particularly valuable?

- Which country would you choose to study in, and why?

Source: HSBC - The Value of Education: Springboard for success
www.hsbc.com

End of
life

Preparing for the end

People are reluctant to talk about dying and they risk leaving it too late to make their wishes known

An online survey of 2,016 British adults aged 18+ revealed that although the majority of people thought it was more acceptable to talk about dying now than it was ten years ago, discussing dying and making end of life plans remains a taboo as many people are uncomfortable discussing dying, death and bereavement.

Which, if any, of the following have you ever done?

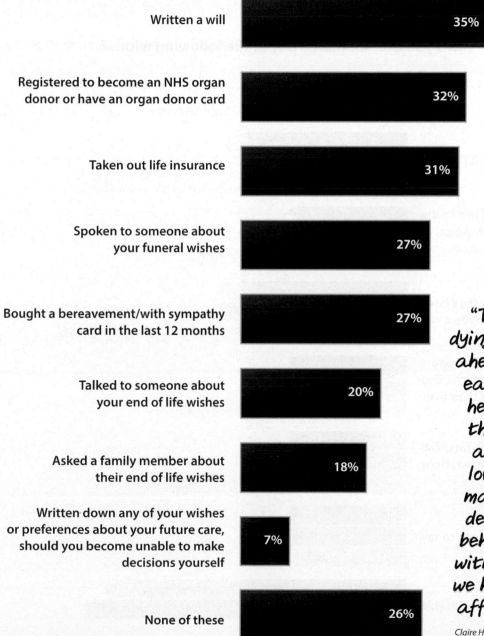

Written a will	35%
Registered to become an NHS organ donor or have an organ donor card	32%
Taken out life insurance	31%
Spoken to someone about your funeral wishes	27%
Bought a bereavement/with sympathy card in the last 12 months	27%
Talked to someone about your end of life wishes	20%
Asked a family member about their end of life wishes	18%
Written down any of your wishes or preferences about your future care, should you become unable to make decisions yourself	7%
None of these	26%

"Talking about dying and planning ahead may not be easy, but it can help us to make the most of life and spare our loved ones from making difficult decisions on our behalf or dealing with the fallout if we haven't got our affairs in order."

Claire Henry, Chief Executive of the Dying Matters Coalition

27%
said they would like to be aged 81-90 when they died

88%
of people overall said they had thought about death

45%
said they thought about death monthly or more

Have you ever discussed any of the following with...?

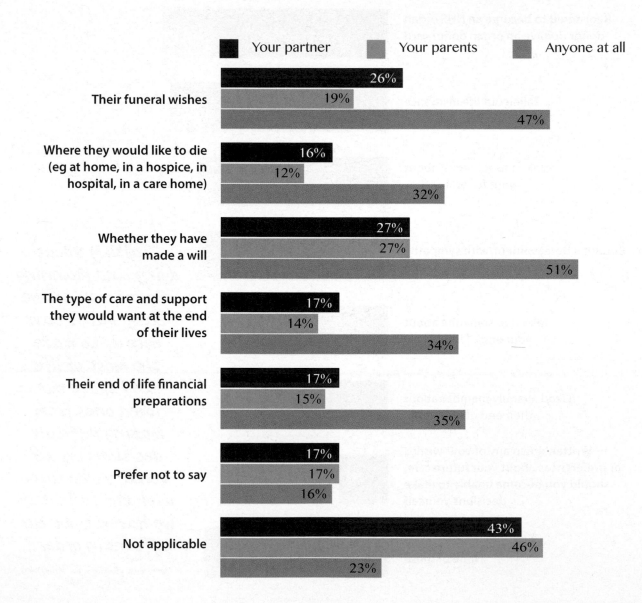

Legend: ■ Your partner ■ Your parents ■ Anyone at all

Their funeral wishes
- Your partner: 26%
- Your parents: 19%
- Anyone at all: 47%

Where they would like to die (eg at home, in a hospice, in hospital, in a care home)
- Your partner: 16%
- Your parents: 12%
- Anyone at all: 32%

Whether they have made a will
- Your partner: 27%
- Your parents: 27%
- Anyone at all: 51%

The type of care and support they would want at the end of their lives
- Your partner: 17%
- Your parents: 14%
- Anyone at all: 34%

Their end of life financial preparations
- Your partner: 17%
- Your parents: 15%
- Anyone at all: 35%

Prefer not to say
- Your partner: 17%
- Your parents: 17%
- Anyone at all: 16%

Not applicable
- Your partner: 43%
- Your parents: 46%
- Anyone at all: 23%

Photo posed by model

"We know that many people have strong views about their end of life wishes, but unless they talk about them and plan ahead they are unlikely to be met."

Professor Mayur Lakhani, a practising GP and Chair of the Dying Matters Coalition

Thinking about your own death are you concerned about the following?

Making adequate financial preparations	**49%**
Family disagreements over money or belongings	**32%**
Their funeral wishes not being followed	**28%**
Lacking capacity to make their own end of life wishes known	**54%**
Their end of life wishes not being met	**43%**

People were asked to rank the following factors in order of how important they were to them to ensure a 'good death' was possible - which factors ranked first

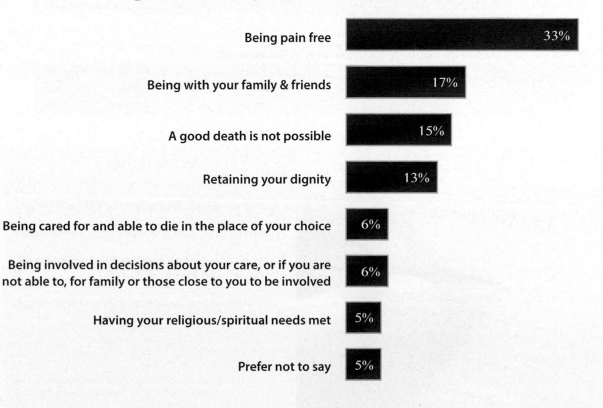

Being pain free	33%
Being with your family & friends	17%
A good death is not possible	15%
Retaining your dignity	13%
Being cared for and able to die in the place of your choice	6%
Being involved in decisions about your care, or if you are not able to, for family or those close to you to be involved	6%
Having your religious/spiritual needs met	5%
Prefer not to say	5%

Thinking about dying, death and bereavement, to what extent, if at all, do you agree or disagree with each of the following statements?

■ Agree   ■ Disagree   ■ Prefer not to say   ■ Don't know

My quality of life is more important to me than how long I live for

| 79% | 6% | 6% | 9% |

I think it is more acceptable to talk about dying, death and bereavement now than it was 10 years ago

| 64% | 13% | 6% | 17% |

If people in Britain felt more comfortable discussing dying, death and bereavement it would be easier to have our end of life wishes met

| 71% | 9% | 6% | 14% |

People in Britain are uncomfortable discussing dying, death and bereavement

| 72% | 12% | 6% | 11% |

Providing end of life care should be a fundamental part of the work of the NHS

| 75% | 8% | 6% | 11% |

End of life care should be a priority for whoever is in Government

| 62% | 17% | 6% | 15% |

Some issues

- Why are we so reluctant to talk about dying?

- What sort of a funeral would you like to have?

- How can we encourage people to prepare for old age and for the end of life?

- At what age should you start to think about death?

*Source: Dying Matters Coalition www.dyingmatters.org
ComRes Death & Dying Survey 2015 www.comres.co.uk*

Assisted dying: public opinion

A vote in Parliament against changing the law on assisted dying seems to be out of step with public opinion

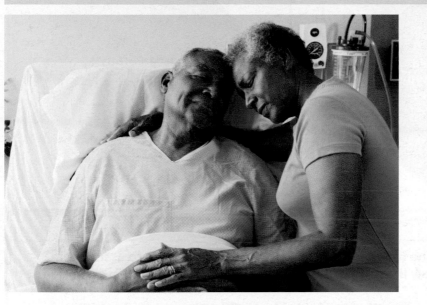

Photo posed by models

Currently it is illegal for a doctor to help someone with a terminal illness to end their life, even if the person considers their suffering unbearable and they are of sound mind.

The penalty for breaking the current law is a maximum sentence of 14 years in prison.

A proposed new law would have allowed terminally ill adults the option of assisted dying. This would mean being provided with life ending medication which they would take themselves. To do this, two doctors would have to agree that they met all of the safeguards:

- The patient would need to be of sound mind;

- be terminally ill;

- have 6 months or less to live;

- a High Court judge would have to be satisfied that this person had made a voluntary, clear and settled decision to end their life, with time to consider all other options.

On 11th September 2015, 74% of MPs voted against the proposed change, (118 were in favour and 330 against).

5,018 GB adults 18+ were asked their opinions about proposed changes in the law and how they think they would act when faced with someone suffering.

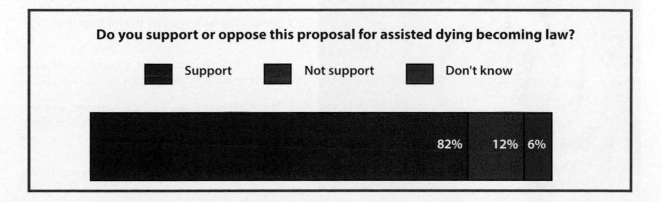

Do you support or oppose this proposal for assisted dying becoming law?

Support   Not support   Don't know

82%   12%   6%

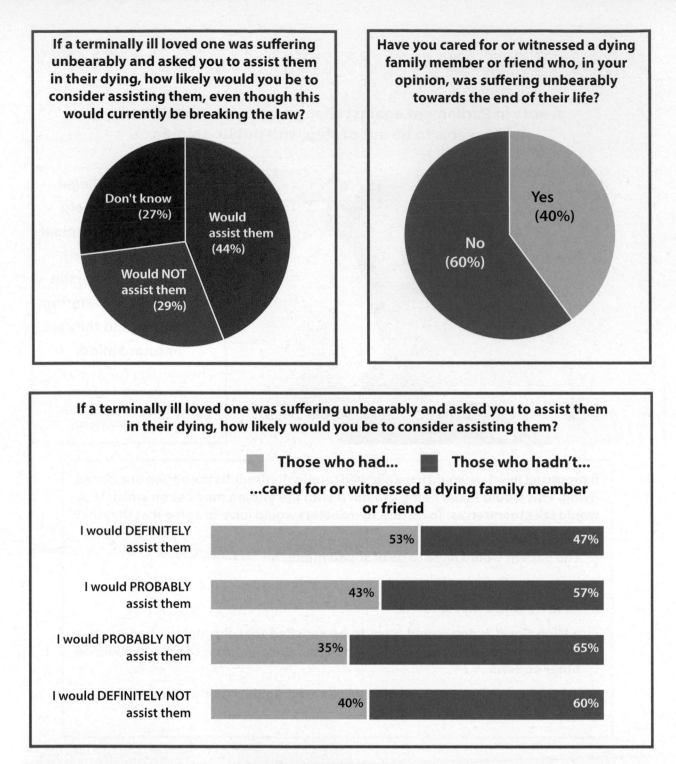

If a terminally ill loved one was suffering unbearably and asked you to assist them in their dying, how likely would you be to consider assisting them, even though this would currently be breaking the law?

Don't know (27%)

Would assist them (44%)

Would NOT assist them (29%)

Have you cared for or witnessed a dying family member or friend who, in your opinion, was suffering unbearably towards the end of their life?

Yes (40%)

No (60%)

If a terminally ill loved one was suffering unbearably and asked you to assist them in their dying, how likely would you be to consider assisting them?

Those who had...   Those who hadn't...

...cared for or witnessed a dying family member or friend

	Those who had...	Those who hadn't...
I would DEFINITELY assist them	53%	47%
I would PROBABLY assist them	43%	57%
I would PROBABLY NOT assist them	35%	65%
I would DEFINITELY NOT assist them	40%	60%

Some issues

- What is your personal opinion on this issue?

- Would the proposal have allowed vulnerable people to be persuaded to end their lives too soon?

- Committing suicide is not a crime, so why is helping someone to commit suicide illegal?

- There seems to be stronger support in the general public than amongst MPs for this proposal. Why might that be?

Source: Populus www.populus.co.uk

Assisted dying: doctors' views

Assisting another person's death is against UK law.
What do doctors think about proposed changes?

A survey by the Royal College of Physicians (RCP) asked doctors about their attitudes to assisted dying. Although views have changed over time, a majority of the hospital doctors they asked still do not support a change in the law

Do you support a change in the law to permit assisted suicide by the terminally ill with the assistance of doctors?
(Base: 6,710)

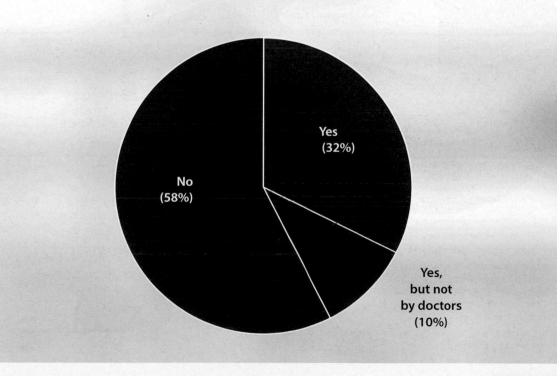

Yes
(32%)

No
(58%)

Yes,
but not
by doctors
(10%)

A comparison with 2006 shows that attitudes have changed.

(Base: 2014- 6,686, 2006 - 5,068)

Do you agree that patients can be cared for properly and can die with dignity under the existing law?

■ Yes   ■ No

2006
- 73.2%
- 26.0%

2014
- 62.5%
- 37.5%

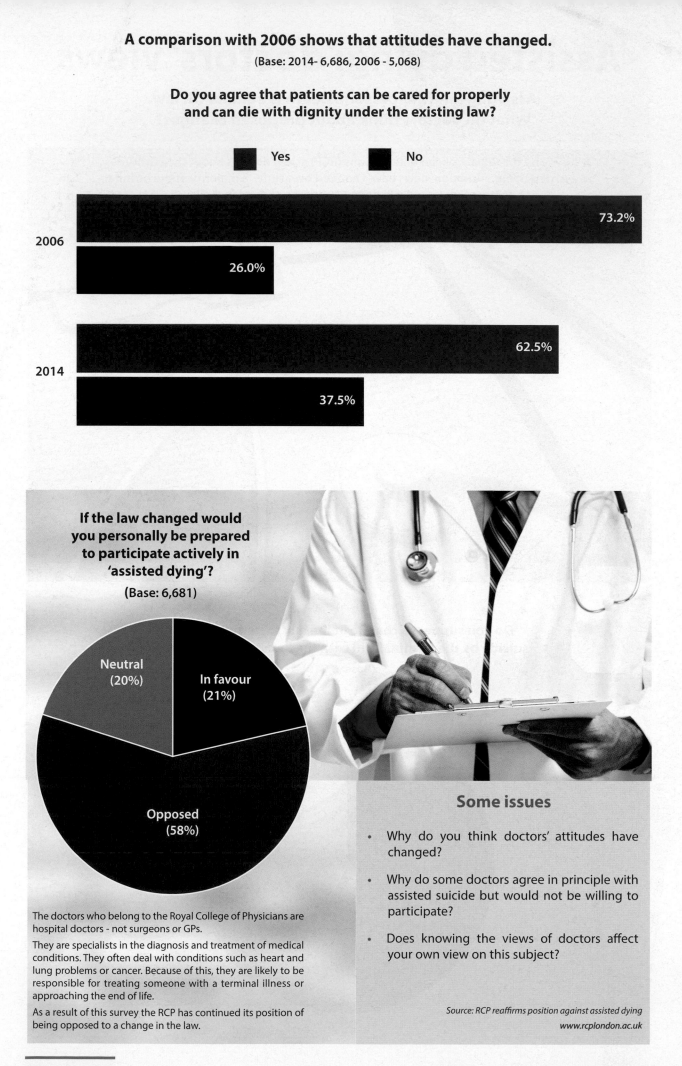

If the law changed would you personally be prepared to participate actively in 'assisted dying'?

(Base: 6,681)

Neutral (20%)

In favour (21%)

Opposed (58%)

The doctors who belong to the Royal College of Physicians are hospital doctors - not surgeons or GPs.

They are specialists in the diagnosis and treatment of medical conditions. They often deal with conditions such as heart and lung problems or cancer. Because of this, they are likely to be responsible for treating someone with a terminal illness or approaching the end of life.

As a result of this survey the RCP has continued its position of being opposed to a change in the law.

Some issues

- Why do you think doctors' attitudes have changed?

- Why do some doctors agree in principle with assisted suicide but would not be willing to participate?

- Does knowing the views of doctors affect your own view on this subject?

Source: RCP reaffirms position against assisted dying
www.rcplondon.ac.uk

Environment

Beach litter

Beach litter is at the highest level since records began

marine conservation society

Every year the Marine Conservation Society organises the Great British Beach Clean, the only national beach litter clean up and survey of its kind in the UK.

Where the litter came from in 2014

All of the litter we find on beaches is preventable - most can be traced back to the general public.

Fishing: 11.09%

eg fishing line, nets, rope, weights, buoys

Sewage related debris: 5.40%

eg cotton bud sticks and sanitary items flushed down the toilet

Public: 38.18%

eg items we drop or leave behind on a trip to the beach or bits carried there by winds and rivers

Shipping: 4.15%

eg items dropped or lost from ships

Fly tipped: 0.98%

eg items illegally disposed of like furniture, pottery and ceramics

Medical: 0.21%

eg inhalers, plasters, syringes

Non-sourced: 40.0%

eg items too small or damaged to identify what they are or where they came from

The percentage of public litter has gone down over the last two years, however the volume has increased – so more items are found in every kilometre cleaned.

During the Great British Beach Clean:

301 beaches were cleaned	**5,349** volunteered	**2,457** pieces of litter were collected per kilometre of beach	**101** different types of litter were recorded

Top 10 litter items found on our beaches per km

Plastic pieces	574.7
Crisp/sweet/ lolly wrappers sandwich wrappers	142.3
Caps/lids	132.4
Polystyrene pieces (under 50cm)	113.6
Glass pieces	104.8
String and cord (under 1cm)	93.1
Cigarette stubs	90.4
Fishing line	77.3
Fishing net (under 50cm)	70.8
Drinks bottles	68.9

Over the last decade almost all the different types of litter found on our beaches have increased. Only a few have gone down - cotton bud sticks and cigarette packets.

The wet wipe problem

Many people think wet wipes, which include moist toilet tissue, are flushable, but they don't break down like toilet tissue because they are made of tougher fibres.

Some even contain plastic such as polyester.

In 2014 the number of wet wipes found on UK beaches **increased** by **more than 50%** compared to 2013 – **35** of them in every kilometre cleaned!

Lit lanterns can cause fires on land and can be mistaken for flares from ships, leading to false alarms for lifeboat and coastguard services.

What happens to our rubbish?

- More and more organisations and individuals are putting marine creatures at risk without realising it. Balloon releases over land eventually drift down into the sea and end up in the gullets of seabirds, turtles and dolphins who mistake them for food.

- Marine wildlife gets entangled in litter and accidentally swallows it. Turtles mistake plastic bags for jellyfish and the bags block their stomachs, often leading to death from starvation.

- Seabirds mistake floating plastic litter for food and over 90% of fulmars found dead around the North Sea have plastic in their stomachs.

- Face scrubs, masks and peels contain tiny plastic particles. They go down the drain and eventually into the sea where they contribute to the 'plastic soup' problem. Microplastic particles are now found inside animals that filter water in order to feed, such as flamingos, clams, and sponges and also amongst sand grains on our beaches.

Since Beachwatch began in 1994...

5.3 million
pieces of litter
weighing over

150 tons
have been collected
from nearly

3,000 km
of beaches.

Plastic litter on beaches has increased
180%.

Some issues

- How can we reduce the amount of litter on our beaches and in our seas?

- Can you, personally, do anything about this problem?

- Apart from collecting up some litter, does a survey like this serve any purpose?

Source: Great British Beach Clean 2014 – Marine Conservation Society
www.mcsuk.org/beachwatch

see also Essential Articles 14, The truth is hard to swallow, p68

Endangered species

Of the 1.5 million species on this planet, 16,118 are endangered

Threatened species can be:

Critically Endangered
A species facing an extremely high risk of extinction in the wild.

Endangered
A species considered to be facing a very high risk of extinction in the wild.

Vulnerable
A species considered to be facing a high risk of extinction in the wild.

African lions
Number remaining:
30,000-35,000

Extinction risk:
Vulnerable

Giant pandas
Number remaining:
Around 1,600

Extinction risk:
Endangered

Amur leopards

Number remaining:
As few as 45

Extinction risk:
Critically endangered

The Amur leopard is probably the rarest and most endangered big cat in the world. Habitat destruction, and poaching of Amur leopards and their prey are persistent threats.

Mountain gorillas

Number remaining:
Around 880

Extinction risk:
Critically endangered

Polar bears

Number remaining:
20,000-25,000

Extinction risk:
Vulnerable

Orang-utans
Number remaining:
52,300- 66,300

Extinction risk:
Endangered - critically endangered

The illegal wildlife trade is one of the biggest dangers to the survival of the world's most threatened species, second only to habitat destruction

Elephants in central Africa could be extinct in our lifetime

African elephant
Number remaining:
Around 600,000

Extinction risk:
Vulnerable

22,000 African elephants were estimated to be killed by poachers for their ivory in 2012.

Tigers
Number remaining:
As few as 3,200

Extinction risk:
Endangered

Between 2000 and 2013, the body parts of at least **1,537** tigers were seized in Asia.

1 rhino killed every 8 hours by poachers in 2014

African rhino

Number remaining:
25,000

Extinction risk:
Near threatened - critically endangered

Number of rhinos killed for their horns in South Africa

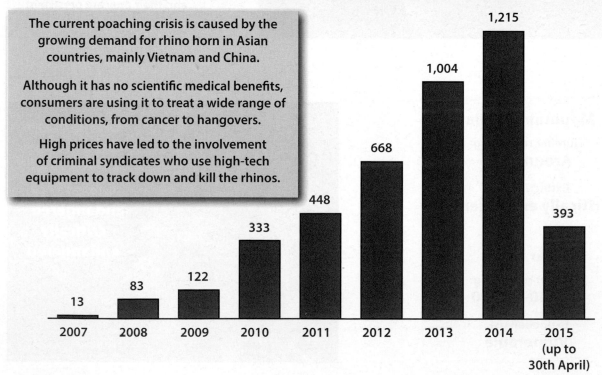

The current poaching crisis is caused by the growing demand for rhino horn in Asian countries, mainly Vietnam and China.

Although it has no scientific medical benefits, consumers are using it to treat a wide range of conditions, from cancer to hangovers.

High prices have led to the involvement of criminal syndicates who use high-tech equipment to track down and kill the rhinos.

Year	Number
2007	13
2008	83
2009	122
2010	333
2011	448
2012	668
2013	1,004
2014	1,215
2015 (up to 30th April)	393

> "It's great to see that nearly 60% of those surveyed were concerned about declining wildlife populations and believe they should do more to protect them."
>
> Rachel Bloodworth Head of Public Engagement at WWF-UK

People may be worried, but many are not well informed

The WWF asked 2,000 adults in the UK about their knowledge of endangered species.

Percentage who mistakenly thought these animals were endangered	
Red Admiral butterfly	38%
Red kangaroo	36%
Swan	28%
Weever fish	28%
Crane fly	21%
Flamingo	20%
Friesian cow	19%
Grey squirrel	19%
Highland cattle	17%

Percentage who mistakenly thought these animals were not endangered	
Fin whale	48%
Green turtle	42%
Asian elephant	37%
Bonobo chimpanzee	35%
Mountain gorilla	26%
Bornean orang-utan	25%
Hawksbill turtle	25%
Snow leopard	22%
Giant panda	17%
Bengal tiger	16%
Black rhino	12%

19% of respondents also listed the dinosaur Brachiosaurus as **endangered**, and **14%** as **not endangered**.

26% thought the Dodo still roamed the planet.

14% of those believed that this flightless bird was currently under threat from hunters ie **endangered**.

In fact it became extinct over 400 years ago.

Some issues

- Why should we care about animals becoming endangered or even extinct?
- Does it matter that people don't realise which animals are endangered?
- Do you know why certain animals are in danger?
- Are there any species you would not want to see saved?
- Whose responsibility is it to make sure that animals are protected?

Source: WWF www.wwf.org.uk
Save the Rhino International
www.savetherhino.org/rhino_info/poaching_statistics

Fracking

What 18-24 year olds think about fracking and other energy sources

What do we know?

Do you know what the term 'fracking' means?

(Base: 1,003 GB 18-24 year olds)

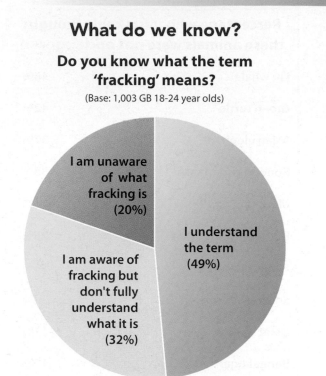

I am unaware of what fracking is (20%)

I am aware of fracking but don't fully understand what it is (32%)

I understand the term (49%)

So what is fracking?

Shale gas is natural gas trapped under sedimentary rock, which is extracted using a method known as hydraulic fracturing, or "fracking". There are large reserves of shale gas in parts of England.

Some people think that using shale gas could be a solution to Britain's energy needs. Other people think that fracking is a dangerous technique that risks contaminating ground water and causing minor earthquakes.

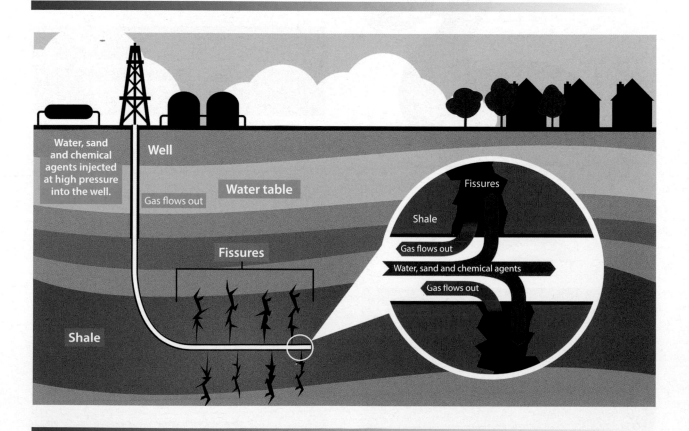

Water, sand and chemical agents injected at high pressure into the well.

Well

Water table

Gas flows out

Fissures

Shale

Fissures

Shale

Gas flows out

Water, sand and chemical agents

Gas flows out

Those repondents who understood or were aware of fracking were asked:

Thinking about your future and future generations, suppose fracking were to be allowed on a large scale in Britain. Do you think it would or would not have each of the following effects?

% who thought that it probably and definitely would (combined)

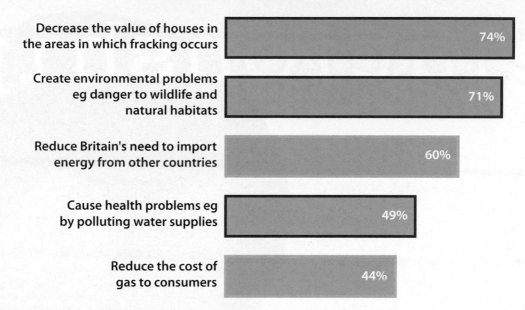

Decrease the value of houses in the areas in which fracking occurs — 74%

Create environmental problems eg danger to wildlife and natural habitats — 71%

Reduce Britain's need to import energy from other countries — 60%

Cause health problems eg by polluting water supplies — 49%

Reduce the cost of gas to consumers — 44%

Those respondents were also asked: "Now suppose a gas company wanted to build a surface site for fracking, typically the size of Trafalgar Square, but would not be drilling underneath your home. What is the closest distance you would be happy for this surface site to be built near your home?"

5% said around half a mile; **10%** said around a mile; **15%** around 2 miles; **19%** around 5 miles; **10%** around 10 miles; but **25%** said they would want to be more than 10 miles away from a fracking site. The remaining **16%** didn't know.

Those repondents were asked:
Overall, which one or two of these sources of energy would you MOST like to see the Government support over the next few years?

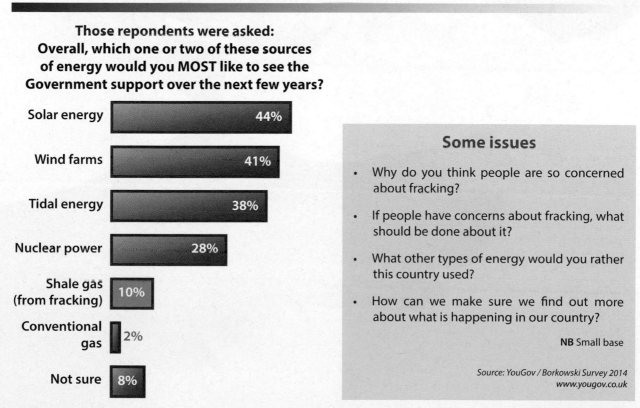

Solar energy — 44%

Wind farms — 41%

Tidal energy — 38%

Nuclear power — 28%

Shale gas (from fracking) — 10%

Conventional gas — 2%

Not sure — 8%

Some issues

- Why do you think people are so concerned about fracking?

- If people have concerns about fracking, what should be done about it?

- What other types of energy would you rather this country used?

- How can we make sure we find out more about what is happening in our country?

NB Small base

Source: YouGov / Borkowski Survey 2014
www.yougov.co.uk

Family & relationships

Parenting

How strict should parents be with their children?

1,741 GB adults were asked about their experiences of family life.

When I was growing up my parents were:

■ Very strict ■ Fairly strict ■ Not very strict ■ Not at all strict ■ Don't know

15%	60%	20%	3%	

2%

Nearly everyone - 92% - who said their own parents were fairly strict said that fairly strict parenting was the best way to raise children.

I personally think it is better if parents are:

■ Very strict ■ Fairly strict ■ Not very strict ■ Not at all strict ■ Don't know

5%	78%	12%	3%	

1%

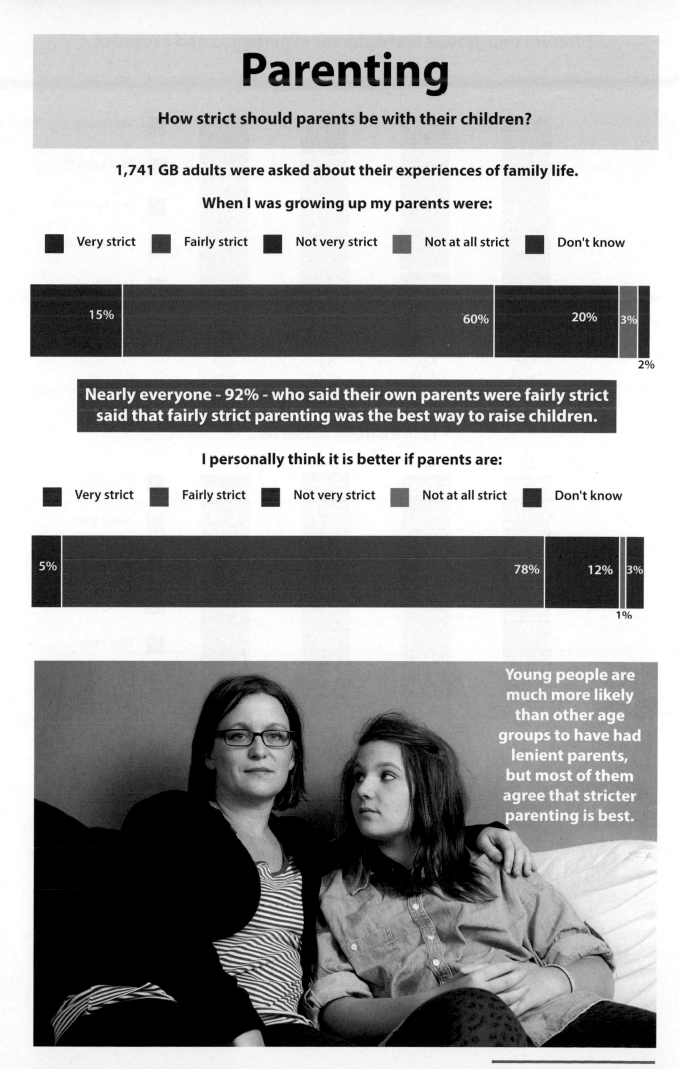

Young people are much more likely than other age groups to have had lenient parents, but most of them agree that stricter parenting is best.

Different age groups had different experiences and attitudes

My parents were....

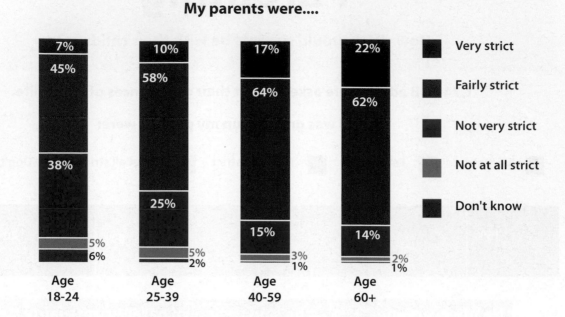

Age 18-24: 7% Very strict, 45% Fairly strict, 38% Not very strict, 5% Not at all strict, 6% Don't know

Age 25-39: 10% Very strict, 58% Fairly strict, 25% Not very strict, 5% Not at all strict, 2% Don't know

Age 40-59: 17% Very strict, 64% Fairly strict, 15% Not very strict, 3% Not at all strict, 1% Don't know

Age 60+: 22% Very strict, 62% Fairly strict, 14% Not very strict, 2% Not at all strict, 1% Don't know

Legend: Very strict · Fairly strict · Not very strict · Not at all strict · Don't know

I think parents should be...

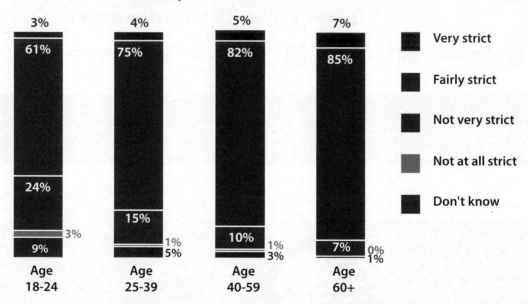

Age 18-24: 3% Very strict, 61% Fairly strict, 24% Not very strict, 3% Not at all strict, 9% Don't know

Age 25-39: 4% Very strict, 75% Fairly strict, 15% Not very strict, 1% Not at all strict, 5% Don't know

Age 40-59: 5% Very strict, 82% Fairly strict, 10% Not very strict, 1% Not at all strict, 3% Don't know

Age 60+: 7% Very strict, 85% Fairly strict, 7% Not very strict, 0% Not at all strict, 1% Don't know

Legend: Very strict · Fairly strict · Not very strict · Not at all strict · Don't know

NB Figures do not add up to 100% due to rounding

When they were growing up...

61% of those asked said they were **friends** with their **mother**

50% said they were **friends** with their **father**.

As an adult...

71% said they were **friends** with their **mother**

64% said they were **friends** with their **father**.

Some issues

- Can you give examples of different levels of strictness?

- Are there some things that parents definitely should be strict about? And others where they could be more relaxed?

- Why do people's views on parenting differ according to how old they are?

- Could you describe a perfect parent?

Source: YouGov yougov.co.uk

Siblings

First borns are sensible, last borns are laid back!

86% of British families have more than one child and there seems to be a clear difference in personality between the first and last born children.

Age itself, rather than family dynamics, could be the cause of these differing characteristics.

As parents shift their attention onto newborns, older siblings may have needed to learn the ropes themselves.

Perhaps because of this they were more likely to feel more organised and able to prioritise their own lives.

1,561 GB adults were asked:
When you were growing up, which characteristics did you display more of than your siblings?

The responses of the youngest and oldest children in the family were compared.

The youngest siblings thought they displayed more of these characteristics

46% of the youngest children

36% of the oldest children

... thought they were more *funny* than their siblings

17% of the youngest children

10% of the oldest children

... thought they were more *favoured by their parents* than their siblings

47% of the youngest children

42% of the oldest children

... thought they were more *easy going* than their siblings

42% of the youngest children

39% of the oldest children

... thought they were more *relaxed* than their siblings

The oldest siblings thought they displayed more of these characteristics

54% of the oldest children

31% of the youngest children

... thought they were more *responsible* than their siblings

38% of the oldest children

24% of the youngest children

... thought they were more *successful* than their siblings

54% of the oldest children

43% of the youngest children

... thought they were more *organised* than their siblings

43% of the oldest children

34% of the youngest children

... thought they were more *able to prioritise their own life* than their siblings

34% of the oldest children

28% of the youngest children

... thought they were more *self-confident* than their siblings

32% of the oldest children

27% of the youngest children

... thought they were more *family orientated* than their siblings

Some issues

- Is this generalisation valid, in your opinion?

- Do middle children have any special characteristics?

- Do you agree with the reasons offered for these different character traits?

- What other aspects of family structure could influence your character?

Source: Ipsos MORI www.ipsos-mori.com

Stresses & strains

UK adults rate family life highly, but there are many external factors putting pressure on it

5,778 adults aged 16+ in England, Scotland, Wales and Northern Ireland were surveyed about their relationships.

They were given a list of 17 life challenges and asked to rank in order the three that placed the most strain on relationships.

Top 10 problems that place a strain on relationships
(does not include those who stated 'Don't know')

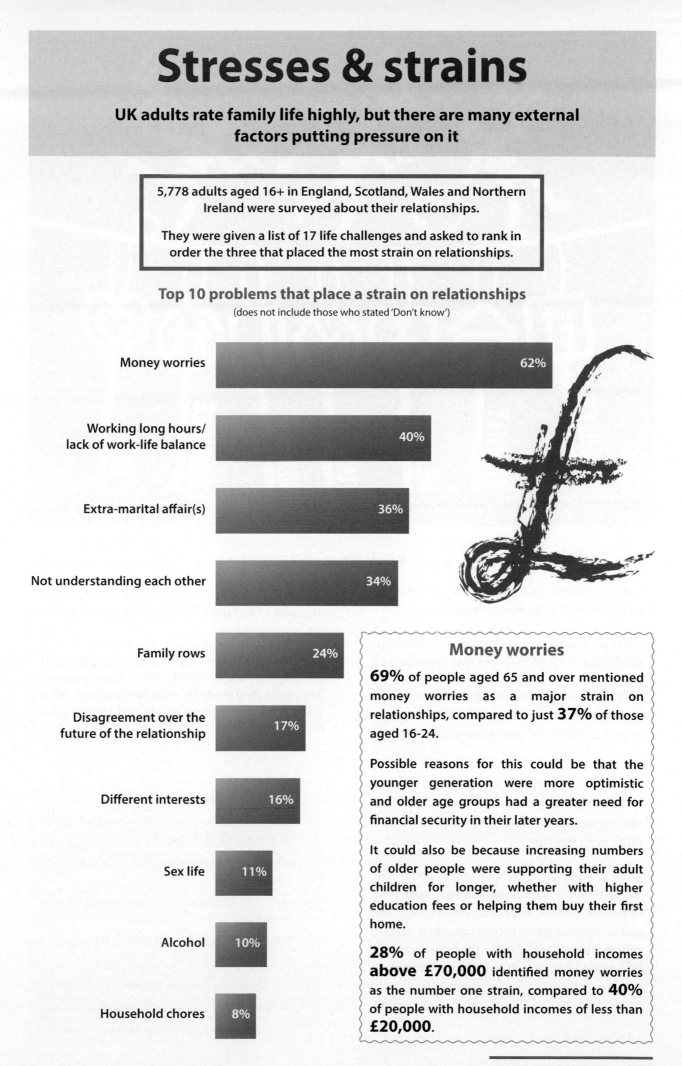

Money worries	62%
Working long hours/ lack of work-life balance	40%
Extra-marital affair(s)	36%
Not understanding each other	34%
Family rows	24%
Disagreement over the future of the relationship	17%
Different interests	16%
Sex life	11%
Alcohol	10%
Household chores	8%

Money worries

69% of people aged 65 and over mentioned money worries as a major strain on relationships, compared to just **37%** of those aged 16-24.

Possible reasons for this could be that the younger generation were more optimistic and older age groups had a greater need for financial security in their later years.

It could also be because increasing numbers of older people were supporting their adult children for longer, whether with higher education fees or helping them buy their first home.

28% of people with household incomes **above £70,000** identified money worries as the number one strain, compared to **40%** of people with household incomes of less than **£20,000**.

Work/life balance

Trying to maintain a good work/life balance was a source of frustration and guilt for many.

20% of people believed their employer would ideally like an employee who was available 24/7.

33% of people believed that their employers thought that the most productive employees were those who put work before their family life.

This rose to **40%** amongst 25-34 year olds but dropped to less than **30%** of people aged 55-64.

Younger people might feel this way because of competing priorities - trying to build a career and get ahead in the workplace while they are at an age where they are likely to be forming long-term relationships, starting a family and setting up a home.

Child care

The increasing cost of child care was also a concern for families.

Among those with children aged under five, **12%** thought that disagreements over child care were a major stress on relationships. This was a much higher proportion than among people with older children - the figure was only **6%** among parents with children aged 5-18.

Some issues

- Do you think the top ten problems are typical of the strains on family life?

- Why would money worries affect people's relationships?

- What can be done to balance family life and work?

- Why is childcare for the under fives such a strain?

Source: Office for National Statistics © Crown copyright 2015
www.ons.gov.uk
The Way We Are Now - The State of the UK's Relationships 2014, Relate
www.relate.org.uk
Relationships Scotland   www.relationships-scotland.org.uk

Looking after children

The number of looked after children has increased steadily over the past five years and it is now higher than at any point since 1985

Children are classed as being 'looked after' if they are aged under 18 and in the care of the local authority.

Why children are looked after

Reasons range from abuse and neglect through to a need to offer parents or children a short break because of severe disability. Children are looked after:

- when a child is living in accommodation provided by the local authority with the parents' agreement ie where parents are struggling to cope;

- when children's services have become involved because a child is at risk of significant harm, ie being ill treated, or the child's health or development is being held back compared to what might be reasonably expected of a similar child;

- a child is the subject of an emergency legal order to remove them from immediate danger;

- a child is serving time in a secure children's home, secure training centre or young offender institution;

- the child is an unaccompanied asylum seeker ie one who has arrived in the UK alone or with a person who is not their usual carer, to claim asylum.

Photo posed by models

The number of children being looked after 2010-2014

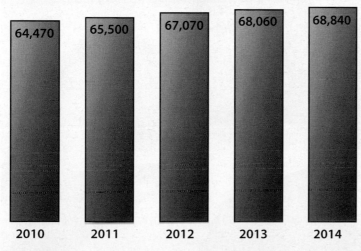

Year	Number
2010	64,470
2011	65,500
2012	67,070
2013	68,060
2014	68,840

Abuse & neglect

The 2014 total: 68,840 is a rate of 60 children for every 10,000

62% of looked after children in 2014 are provided with a service due to abuse or neglect.

Children in the care of local authorities on 31st March 2014 ...

...by gender

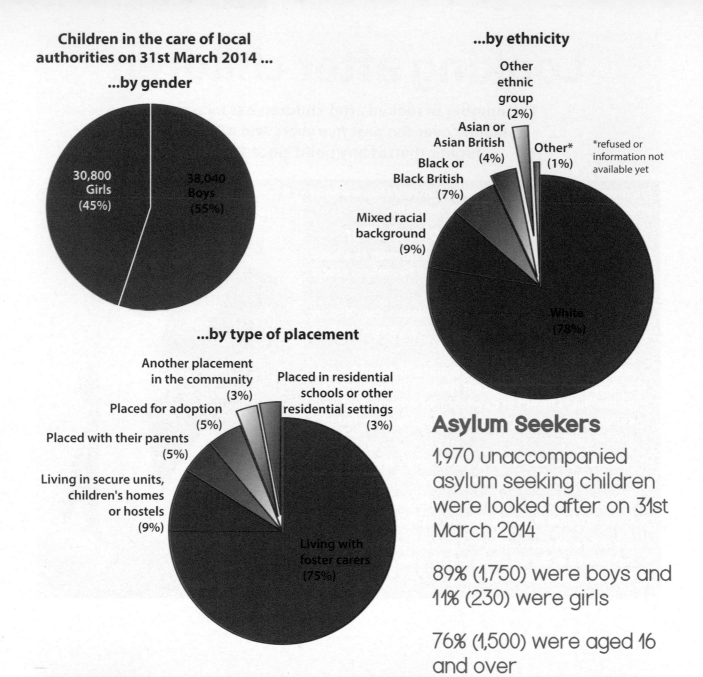

30,800 Girls (45%)

38,040 Boys (55%)

...by ethnicity

Other ethnic group (2%)

Asian or Asian British (4%)

Other* (1%)

*refused or information not available yet

Black or Black British (7%)

Mixed racial background (9%)

White (78%)

...by type of placement

Another placement in the community (3%)

Placed in residential schools or other residential settings (3%)

Placed for adoption (5%)

Placed with their parents (5%)

Living in secure units, children's homes or hostels (9%)

Living with foster carers (75%)

Asylum Seekers

1,970 unaccompanied asylum seeking children were looked after on 31st March 2014

89% (1,750) were boys and 11% (230) were girls

76% (1,500) were aged 16 and over

Foster care

51,340 children were cared for in a foster placement. This represents an increase of **9%** since 2010, a larger increase than the rise in overall numbers of looked after children.

Photo posed by models

Who was adopted?

5,050 children were adopted from care during the year ending 31st March 2014. There was an equal numbers of boys and girls.

This was an increase of **58%** since 2010 and was the highest number since the start of this data collection in 1992.

Who is adopting?

91% (**4,610**) of children were adopted by couples and **9%** (**440**) by single adopters.

7% (**340**) of children were adopted by same sex couples (either in a civil partnership or not), up from **6%** (**230**) children in the previous year.

A CHILD'S JOURNEY THROUGH ADOPTION

TOTAL 28 Months*

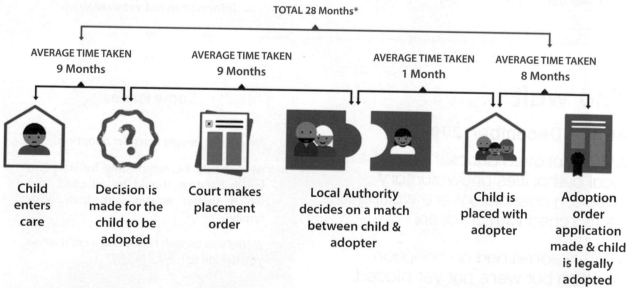

| AVERAGE TIME TAKEN 9 Months | | AVERAGE TIME TAKEN 9 Months | | AVERAGE TIME TAKEN 1 Month | | AVERAGE TIME TAKEN 8 Months | |

Child enters care

Decision is made for the child to be adopted

Court makes placement order

Local Authority decides on a match between child & adopter

Child is placed with adopter

Adoption order application made & child is legally adopted

*This illustrates the key stages of the child's journey from entering care to an adoption court order with average times based on children who were adopted over the year from 1 April 2013 to 31 March 2014. Figures are rounded to the nearest month. Total may not be equal to the sum of breakdowns due to rounding.

Data source: DfE annual SSDA903 data

More than 90% of people say they have one good friend

Friendship and gender

Men were more likely than women to have a higher number of close friends – **5%** of men said they had 15 or more close friends compared to just **2%** of women.

On the other hand, men were also more likely to have no close friends - **11%** of men said they had no close friends compared to **7%** of women.

81% of women describe their friendships as **good or very good** compared to **73%** of men.

Men are more likely to be members of a **group** of close friends, whilst women are more likely to form closer connections with their **individual** friends.

Women's friendships seemed to get better as they aged – **25%** of women aged 16-24 described their relationships with their friends as very good and rose to **60%** of women aged 65 and over.

Men's views about the quality of their friendships stayed relatively constant across the different age groups.

Which age group has the most friends?

In 2014 **3.4%** of people said they had a high number of close friends - **15 or more**.

Young people have plenty of opportunities to make new friends and are likely to make use of social networking, so it is not surprising that **5.4%** of those aged 16-24 have **15 or more** close friends

But older people – those aged 65 and over – were almost as likely as young people to report very high numbers of close friends - **4.4%** reported **15 or more** close friends.

Some issues

- What qualities do you look for in a friend?

- Is '15 close friends' a large number?

- Is it better to have the same group of friends all the time or different groups who share different interests?

- Why do you think older people are almost as likely as the youngest age group to have large groups of friends?

Source: The Way We Are Now - The State of the UK's Relationships 2014, Relate www.relate.org.uk
Relationships Scotland www.relationships-scotland.org.uk

Finance

Unequal shares

How the world's wealth is divided up

Oxfam used data from the financial company Credit Suisse to show that **1%** of people had **48%** of the world's net wealth. (Net wealth is the value of everything you own, minus your debts).

This **1%** amounts to **47 million people** worldwide.

To be in the **1%** you would need to have a net wealth of **£473,000**. Someone who owned an average house in London - worth **£501,500** in 2014 - and didn't have any debts would be in the **1%**.

Share of global wealth of the top 1% and the rest of the world, 2014

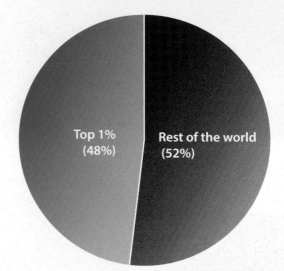

Top 1% (48%)

Rest of the world (52%)

The richest 1% are not evenly distributed through the regions of the world. As might be expected, they are mainly located in the developed countries.

Number of people in the top 1%, by region
(NB Figures are rounded)

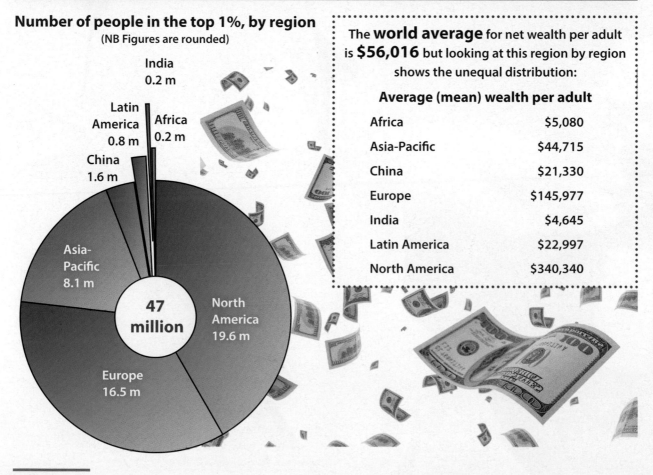

India 0.2 m

Latin America 0.8 m

Africa 0.2 m

China 1.6 m

Asia-Pacific 8.1 m

47 million

North America 19.6 m

Europe 16.5 m

The **world average** for net wealth per adult is **$56,016** but looking at this region by region shows the unequal distribution:

Average (mean) wealth per adult

Africa	$5,080
Asia-Pacific	$44,715
China	$21,330
Europe	$145,977
India	$4,645
Latin America	$22,997
North America	$340,340

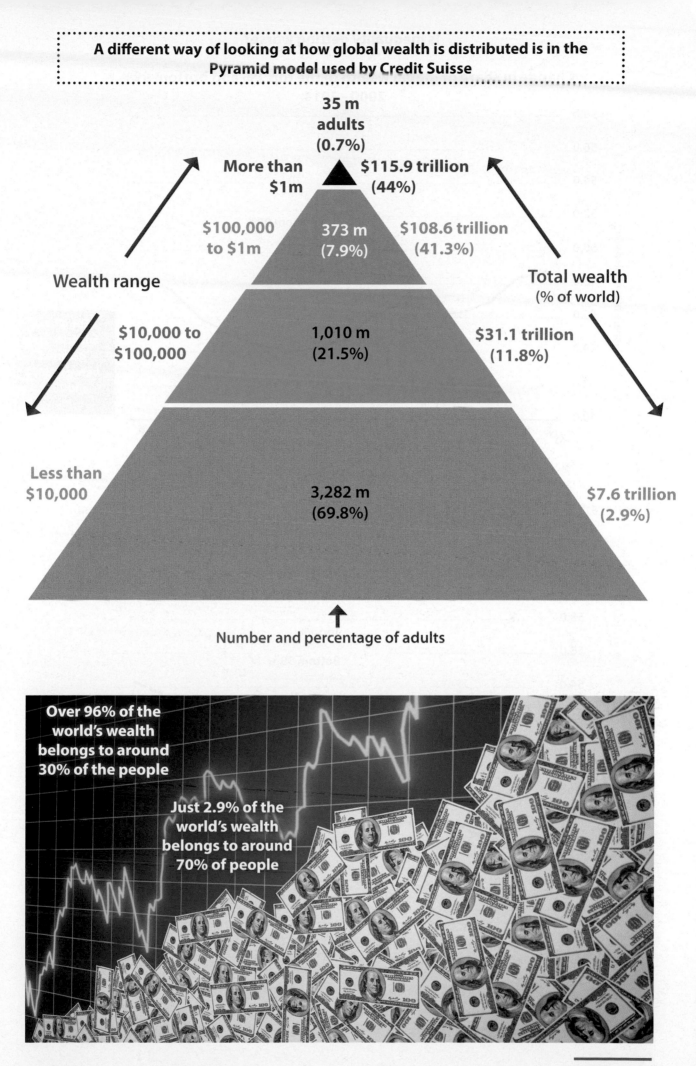

35 m adults (0.7%)

More than $1m

$115.9 trillion (44%)

$100,000 to $1m

373 m (7.9%)

$108.6 trillion (41.3%)

Wealth range

Total wealth (% of world)

$10,000 to $100,000

1,010 m (21.5%)

$31.1 trillion (11.8%)

Less than $10,000

3,282 m (69.8%)

$7.6 trillion (2.9%)

Number and percentage of adults

Over 96% of the world's wealth belongs to around 30% of the people

Just 2.9% of the world's wealth belongs to around 70% of people

Is inequality getting worse?

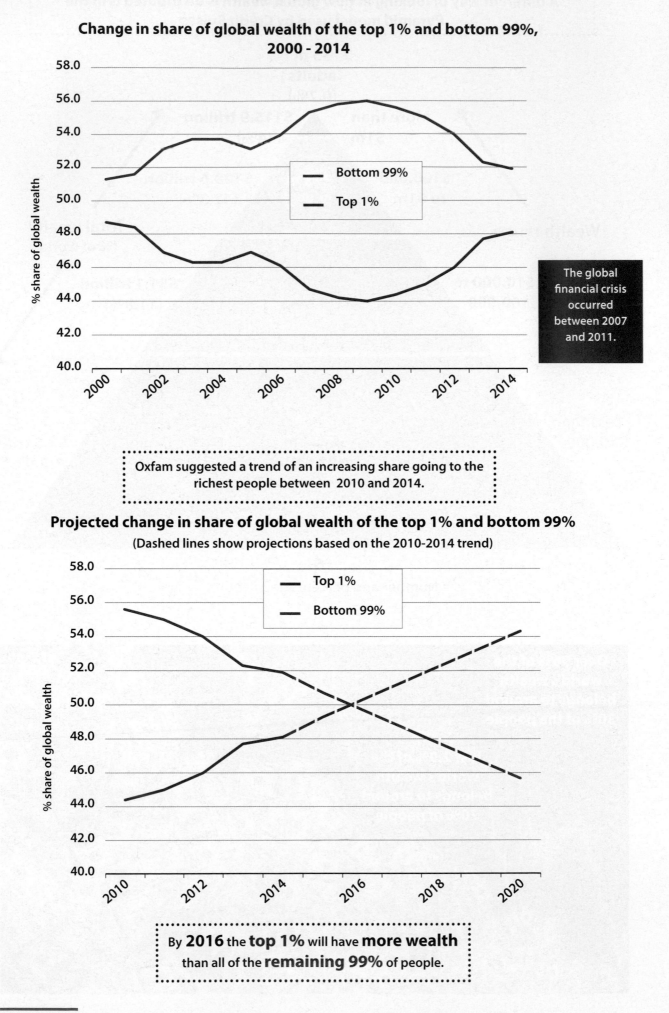

Change in share of global wealth of the top 1% and bottom 99%, 2000 - 2014

Legend:
- Bottom 99%
- Top 1%

The global financial crisis occurred between 2007 and 2011.

Oxfam suggested a trend of an increasing share going to the richest people between 2010 and 2014.

Projected change in share of global wealth of the top 1% and bottom 99%

(Dashed lines show projections based on the 2010-2014 trend)

Legend:
- Top 1%
- Bottom 99%

By **2016** the **top 1%** will have **more wealth** than all of the **remaining 99%** of people.

The very richest people have seen their wealth mount up even faster between 2000 and 2014. The wealth of the 80 richest individuals is now the same as that owned by the bottom 50% of the global population. This means that these extremely wealthy 80 people. share between them the same amount of wealth as 3.5 billion people.

Wealth of the 80 richest people in the world and wealth of the bottom 50%

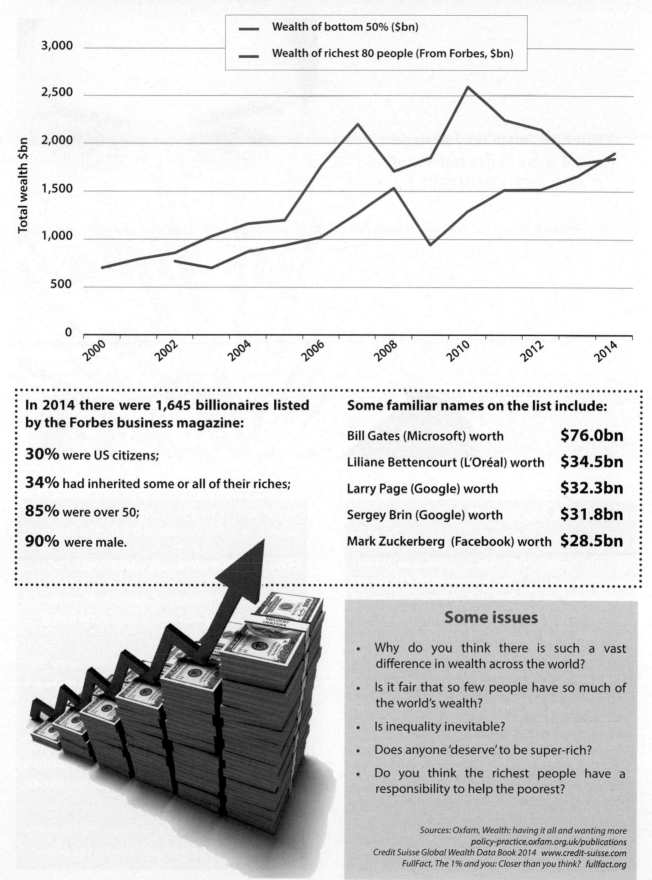

Legend:
— Wealth of bottom 50% ($bn)
— Wealth of richest 80 people (From Forbes, $bn)

Y-axis: Total wealth $bn (0, 500, 1,000, 1,500, 2,000, 2,500, 3,000)
X-axis: 2000, 2002, 2004, 2006, 2008, 2010, 2012, 2014

In 2014 there were 1,645 billionaires listed by the Forbes business magazine:

30% were US citizens;

34% had inherited some or all of their riches;

85% were over 50;

90% were male.

Some familiar names on the list include:

Bill Gates (Microsoft) worth	**$76.0bn**
Liliane Bettencourt (L'Oréal) worth	**$34.5bn**
Larry Page (Google) worth	**$32.3bn**
Sergey Brin (Google) worth	**$31.8bn**
Mark Zuckerberg (Facebook) worth	**$28.5bn**

Some issues

- Why do you think there is such a vast difference in wealth across the world?
- Is it fair that so few people have so much of the world's wealth?
- Is inequality inevitable?
- Does anyone 'deserve' to be super-rich?
- Do you think the richest people have a responsibility to help the poorest?

Sources: Oxfam, Wealth: having it all and wanting more
policy-practice.oxfam.org.uk/publications
Credit Suisse Global Wealth Data Book 2014 www.credit-suisse.com
FullFact, The 1% and you: Closer than you think? fullfact.org

Super rich

To be in the richest 1% of the WORLD, it's best to be born in a rich country...

...But how much do you need to earn to be in the top 1% of each RICH COUNTRY?

How is this calculated?

An economist, Branko Milanovic, has worked out the average earnings of a person in each country's top 1%. The figures were calculated after taxes were taken out and were adjusted for the cost of living. They are adjusted for the fact that local goods and services are more expensive in some places than others - this is called purchasing power parity (PPP).

Milanovic did not include income from stocks and shares and property sales which actually adds a lot more to the income of some people, an extra third in America.

The chart shows that the top 1% make between **$70,000** and **$170,000** in rich countries. The figures do not take into account other aspects of the cost of living such as the fact that health care is free in many countries but very expensive in others such as the United States

Why is there so much variation?

It's not just a matter of how much income a country has, but also how evenly distributed, or not, that income is.

Brazil for example has so much inequality that its top 1% make more than the top 1% in Italy, a much richer country.

But, you don't need to be anywhere close to your country's top 1% to be in the world's top 1% - the poorest Germans are still better off than **40%** of Brazilians, **60%** of Chinese and **more than 90%** of Indians.

It takes just **$43,000** in PPP terms to be better off than **99%** of everybody else on the planet.

What the richest 1% make in 25 countries

The average earnings per person of a member of the top 1%
(adjusted for the purchasing power of money in those countries)

Country	Earnings
Switzerland	171,832
Australia	157,517
United States	151,534
France	123,760
Luxembourg	119,157
Great Britain	118,836
Canada	115,621
Austria	108,823
Norway	107,290
Czech Republic	101,745
Denmark	99,478
New Zealand	96,211
Germany	95,150
Israel	88,235
Finland	87,206
Chile	84,438
Netherlands	83,462
Iceland	82,743
Taiwan	80,482
Brazil	75,279
Italy	74,134
Greece	71,769
Russia	47,083
South Africa	46,484
Poland	46,371

Some issues

- Is it better to have a low taxes and therefore keep more of your wages or high taxes and more social spending?

- Can anything be done about inequality within countries?

- Should anything be done about inequality between countries? If so, who should do this?

Source: Luxembourg Income Study database,
LIS Cross-National Data Center www.lisdatacenter.org
Washington Post www.washingtonpost.com

High street shops

Online sales and changing consumer demand are leading to store closures

Nearly three times as many shops disappeared in 2014 compared to 2013 - that's equivalent to 16 stores closing per day.

English Regions/UK Countries	Number of store closures	Number of store openings	2014 net change
East Midlands	446	299	-147
East of England	450	418	-32
Greater London	1,386	1,303	-83
North East	213	149	-64
North West	542	410	-132
South East	862	787	-75
South West	521	444	-77
West Midlands	524	371	-153
Yorkshire & the Humber	424	305	-119
Scotland	312	246	-66
Wales	159	120	-39
Total	**5,839**	**4,852**	**-987**

Number of multiple retailer* stores closures and openings, by region across the top 500 GB town centres

In 2014:

- 765 of the more traditional type shops such as clothes and shoe shops closed;

- there was a net decline of -457 service retail shops such as opticians, travel agents, hairdressers and recruitment agencies;

- there were an additional 233 leisure stores such as food, beverage and entertainment type shops.

- charity shops, coffee shops, tobacconists/ E-cigarettes, pound shops and betting shops were among those opening the most branches.

*Multiples are retailers that have more than 5 outlets nationally

Difference between number of stores opening and closing in 2014
(percentage net change in brackets)

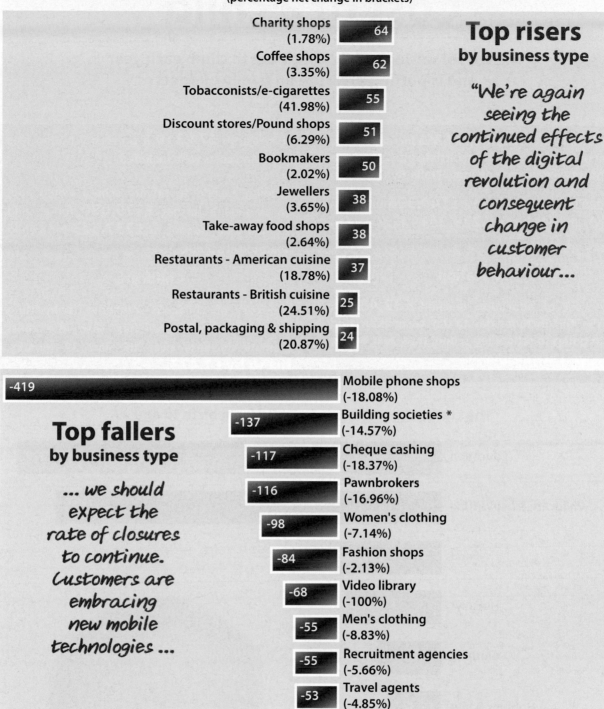

Charity shops
(1.78%)
64

Coffee shops
(3.35%)
62

Tobacconists/e-cigarettes
(41.98%)
55

Discount stores/Pound shops
(6.29%)
51

Bookmakers
(2.02%)
50

Jewellers
(3.65%)
38

Take-away food shops
(2.64%)
38

Restaurants - American cuisine
(18.78%)
37

Restaurants - British cuisine
(24.51%)
25

Postal, packaging & shipping
(20.87%)
24

Top risers
by business type

"We're again seeing the continued effects of the digital revolution and consequent change in customer behaviour..."

-419
Mobile phone shops
(-18.08%)

Top fallers
by business type

... we should expect the rate of closures to continue. Customers are embracing new mobile technologies ...

-137
Building societies *
(-14.57%)

-117
Cheque cashing
(-18.37%)

-116
Pawnbrokers
(-16.96%)

-98
Women's clothing
(-7.14%)

-84
Fashion shops
(-2.13%)

-68
Video library
(-100%)

-55
Men's clothing
(-8.83%)

-55
Recruitment agencies
(-5.66%)

-53
Travel agents
(-4.85%)

*The vast majority of building societies highlighted in these **top fallers** are Britannia bank branches reclassified as building society outlets. In classifying Britannia as building societies it must be noted that some closed and some transferred to Co-op Bank.

Some issues

- If you look at the type of shops that are 'risers' and 'fallers' what conclusions would you draw about the way we live?

- Video library shops have declined by 100%. What sort of shops do you think will be the next to go?

- Does it matter if we have fewer shops on our High Streets?

Those who have grown up with online shopping, mobile phones and broadband have a very different relationship with traditional high streets than the previous generations."

Mark Hudson, retail leader at PwC

*Sources: PwC UK www.pwc.co.uk
Local Data Company www.localdatacompany.com*

Cost of a child

The cost of raising a child continues to climb each year and is putting pressure on family budgets

Since 2003 there has been a **63%** increase in the cost of raising a child from birth to age 21 - that's almost twice the rate of annual inflation.

In 2003 it would have cost **£140,398** to raise a child - in 2015 it cost **£229,251** - equivalent to around **£30 a day**.

Education

The cost of education reached **£32,483** in 2015 - this includes day to day costs associated with going to school (eg school trips, text books, uniform and school lunch).

This rose to **£74,319** if university tuition fees and living costs were included.

Sending a child to private school would add, on average a further **£129,030** for a child attending day school, or **£237,323** for a child boarding at school.

Childcare

The cost of childcare (nurseries, babysitting and after-school care) has seen the most dramatic increase over the last 12 months, **rising by £1,473**.

The current cost of raising a child from birth to age 21

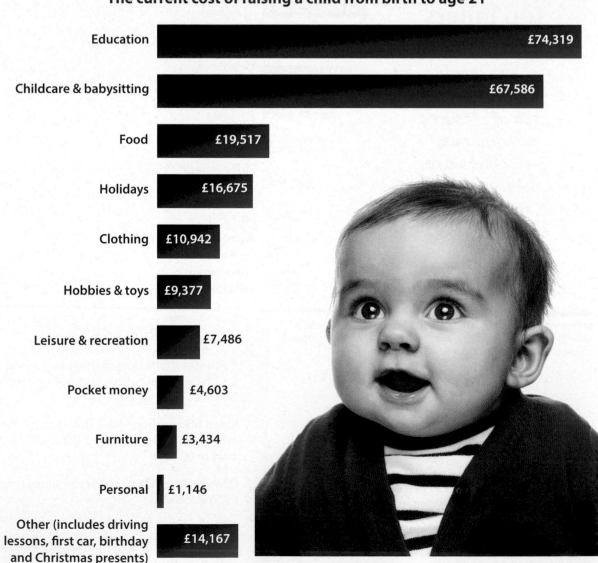

Education	£74,319
Childcare & babysitting	£67,586
Food	£19,517
Holidays	£16,675
Clothing	£10,942
Hobbies & toys	£9,377
Leisure & recreation	£7,486
Pocket money	£4,603
Furniture	£3,434
Personal	£1,146
Other (includes driving lessons, first car, birthday and Christmas presents)	£14,167

Which are the most expensive years?

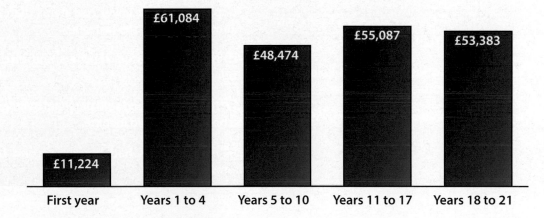

First year	Years 1 to 4	Years 5 to 10	Years 11 to 17	Years 18 to 21
£11,224	£61,084	£48,474	£55,087	£53,383

Differences in cost

The early years of a child's life are the most expensive.

Parents with children aged under three can expect to spend **27%** of their household income on nursery costs.

There's a great difference in the cost of childcare across the UK from the highest, **£81,276** in **London**, to the lowest, **£61,397** in **Yorkshire & Humberside**.

Family size

Rising costs are affecting the size of families - recent figures from the Office for National Statistics predict that by 2022, half of all UK families will have just one child.

- **9%** of parents admit that they are postponing having more children due to financial concerns.

- **11%** of parents have decided to have a smaller family than originally planned due to costs.

- **26%** of younger parents - aged 18-34 - are delaying growing their family.

Higher education

The cost of education has increased by **128%** since the first Cost of a Child report in 2003.

45% of parents felt that university might no longer be an option for their child, either because they thought they wouldn't be able to afford it, or the course wouldn't be worth it.

Overall, **35%** of parents said they worried about university costs.

16% of parents might have to defer sending their child to university for a year or longer to save more.

Cutting back

- **39%** of parents made cuts to spending on clothes.

- **33%** made spending cuts on holidays.

- **23%** said they spent less money on luxury gifts and evenings out than they used to.

- Spending on leisure and recreational activities fell by **27%**.

- **63%** said that when they did the household shop they bought lower cost items than they normally did over the last year.

- **49%** regularly used vouchers and discount codes.

- **37%** of parents had sold personal belongings to boost household income.

- **34%** of parents had bought second hand items.

Work

52% of parents had either had to return to work earlier than planned, or had to take on extra work to make ends meet.

20% of mothers had to return to work from parental leave earlier than planned for financial reasons.

26% of parents had to take a part time job.

15% had to return to full time work rather than part time as they'd preferred.

13% had to work more hours than preferred.

Some issues

- Is it appropriate to include costs up to age 21?

- Why do years 1-4 cost most?

- In your opinion, have costs increased because of prices or because young people expect more to be spent on them?

- Should the decision to have children be based on cost?

Base: Survey of 2,003 UK adults by Opinium Research for LV=

Source: LV= Cost of a child - from cradle to college, 2015 www.lv.com

Food & drink

Emergency food

Families are struggling to make ends meet, but there is still a social stigma in using foodbanks

Foodbanks are a relatively recent phenomenon in Britain. The Trussell Trust charity partners with churches and communities to open new foodbanks nationwide. It launched its first food bank in 1999 and established its network in 2004.

Since then, there has been a big increase in the numbers of emergency food assistance providers, such as Meals on Wheels and soup kitchens. There are around **800** foodbanks across the UK, over half of these are provided by the Trussell Trust.

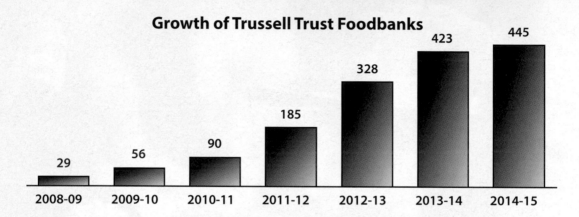

Growth of Trussell Trust Foodbanks

Year	Number
2008-09	29
2009-10	56
2010-11	90
2011-12	185
2012-13	328
2013-14	423
2014-15	445

How a foodbank works

Food is donated:
Schools, churches, businesses and individuals donate non-perishable, in-date food to a foodbank. Large collections often take place as part of Harvest Festival celebrations.

Food is collected at 'Supermarket Collections':
These are events held at supermarkets where volunteers give shoppers a 'foodbank shopping list' and ask them to buy an extra item or two for local people in crisis.

Food is sorted and stored:
Volunteers sort food to check that it's in date and pack it into boxes ready to be given to people in need.

Around **42,000** people volunteered with a foodbank in 2014/15.

Foodbank Shopping list

Milk (UHT or powdered)	Rice pudding (tinned)
Sugar (500g)	Tea Bags / instant coffee
Fruit juice (carton)	Instant mash potato
Soup	Rice / pasta
Pasta sauces	Tinned meat / fish
Sponge pudding (tinned)	Tinned fruit
Tomatoes (tinned)	Jam
Cereals	Biscuits or snack bar

Who do foodbanks help?

People in need:

According to the Trussell Trust, most foodbank clients are low income families who have been hit by a crisis that is not their fault such as redundancy, reduced working hours or even an unexpected bill.

Others are victims of domestic violence, people experiencing benefit delay or facing debt problems or illness.

Identifying people in need:

Foodbank providers consult with frontline professionals such as doctors, health visitors, social workers etc who are best placed to assess need and make sure that it is genuine. Those in need are issued with a foodbank voucher.

34,883 professionals gave out foodbank vouchers in 2014-15.

"There are people out there more desperate than me. I've got a sofa to sell before I'll go to the foodbank. It's a pride thing. You don't want people to know you're on benefits."

A mum who was skipping meals to feed her children

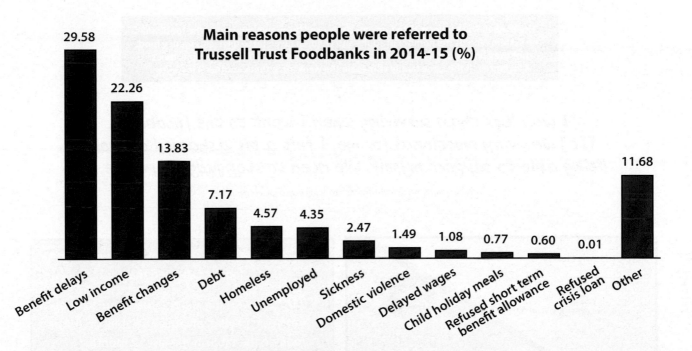

Main reasons people were referred to Trussell Trust Foodbanks in 2014-15 (%)

- Benefit delays: 29.58
- Low income: 22.26
- Benefit changes: 13.83
- Debt: 7.17
- Homeless: 4.57
- Unemployed: 4.35
- Sickness: 2.47
- Domestic violence: 1.49
- Delayed wages: 1.08
- Child holiday meals: 0.77
- Refused short term benefit allowance: 0.60
- Refused crisis loan: 0.01
- Other: 11.68

How foodbank vouchers are used

Foodbank clients bring their voucher to a foodbank centre - one voucher provides a minimum of three days' emergency food.

On average people needed *two* foodbank vouchers in a year.

Some foodbanks also run a delivery service, which takes emergency foodboxes to clients living in rural areas who cannot afford to get to a foodbank.

Photo: Trussell Trust

Numbers* given 3 days' emergency food by Trussell foodbanks

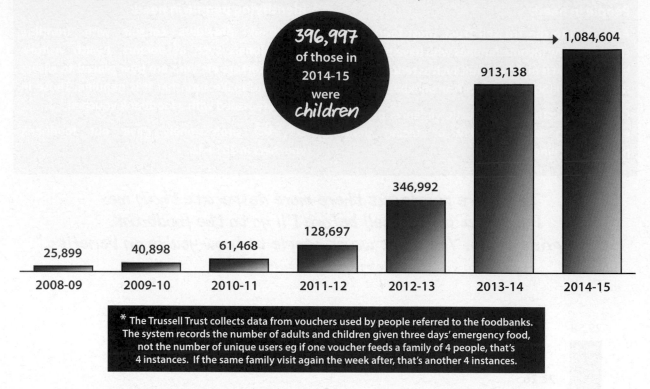

396,997 of those in 2014-15 were *children*

Year	Number
2008-09	25,899
2009-10	40,898
2010-11	61,468
2011-12	128,697
2012-13	346,992
2013-14	913,138
2014-15	1,084,604

* The Trussell Trust collects data from vouchers used by people referred to the foodbanks. The system records the number of adults and children given three days' emergency food, not the number of unique users eg if one voucher feeds a family of 4 people, that's 4 instances. If the same family visit again the week after, that's another 4 instances.

"I was less than surviving when I went to the foodbank. [It] was very emotional for me, I felt a bit ashamed at not being able to support myself. We need to stop judging people..."

Marcella, former dental assistant recovering from a spinal operation

A foodbank client

A 2014 Netmums survey of 2,178 working families showed that:

- **20%** of working parents had had to choose between paying an essential bill or putting food on the table in the last 12 months;
- **78%** of parents in working families had cut spending over the last 12 months;
- **56%** admitted to having to buy cheaper, lower quality food;
- **43%** of those surveyed admitted that they were only 'just about coping' with balancing their family budgets; and
- **25%** stated they have suffered stress as a result of not eating properly.

Despite this, only **1 in 40** had turned to a foodbank for help, with **more than 70%** saying that they would only do so as a **last resort.**

"If there was no foodbank I'd have to steal something to feed my family."

Jamie, Andover Foodbank client

Supermarket waste v public donations

Over 90% of food given out by Trussell Trust foodbanks is donated by the UK public, donating *10,280 tonnes* of food in 2014/15.

In the United States, food donors and organisations that distribute donated food are protected from civil and criminal liability for any harm caused by that food by the *Good Samaritan Food Donation Act.*

Many food providers do not provide their waste food to foodbanks etc because they are concerned that they might be sued if someone gets sick from eating it.

Joint written evidence from food banks in Oxfordshire

[Having] no Good Samaritan Laws in the UK make it legally more attractive to dump rather than donate.

Written evidence from Bruce Marquart, The Upper Room, London

French supermarkets will be banned from throwing away or destroying unsold food and must instead donate it to charities or for animal feed, under a law set to cut down on food waste.

Those with a footprint of 400 sq m or more will have to sign contracts with charities by July 2016 or face penalties including fines of up to €75,000 (£53,000) or two years in jail.

*Foodbank numbers are an inadequate indicator of need, because many households only ask for emergency food help as a **last resort**...*

We view the rise of food poverty as an indication of the reversal of what was a long process of improvement in food availability and affordability since World War Two.

Written evidence from the Faculty of Public Health at the Royal Colleges of Physicians in the United Kingdom

Some issues

- Why do you think more people are using food banks?

- Should supermarkets donate their usable food to food banks?

- Does government have a duty to see that all citizens have an adequate amount of food?

Source: The Trussell Trust www.trusselltrust.org

An Evidence Review for the All-Party Parliamentary Inquiry into Hunger in the United Kingdom www.foodpovertyinquiry.org

Cooking skills

Are we in danger of losing our basic cooking skills?

Research by Love Food Hate Waste & Mumsnet suggests that we are at risk of losing valuable cooking skills and knowledge to pass on to the next generation because our busy lives push us towards quick solutions to preparing meals.

91% of parents thinks cooking skills are an important part of their child's education.

Despite how important parents think cooking is:

61% of parents (with children over the age of three) spend two hours or less a month cooking with their child. Sometimes life can just get too busy.

39% of people say that the speed of preparation is one of the most important things they consider – which could often mean missing out on homemade meals.

We've become too busy to cook

Lack of food knowledge and cooking skills can be bad for our health, while having these skills can save us money and help to reduce food waste.

Building skills in the kitchen is vital if the UK is to tackle the **£12.5 billion** of good food and drink that gets thrown away from homes each year.

34% say that one of the most important things they consider when planning a meal is how to use up food that's nearing its best before date.

28% say that when it comes to making the most of food, the one tip they'd pass on to their children is how to cook with leftovers.

45% say that, to help their children make the most out of food, they'll teach them how to plan meals.

Some issues

- How often do you and your family cook a meal from 'scratch'?

- Does it really matter if people don't know how to cook?

- How much food do you think your family wastes each week?

- What can you do to waste less food?

Source: Love Food Hate Waste england.lovefoodhatewaste.com

Local produce

People's attitudes to buying food and drink produced or grown in their own country or region

2,064 GB adults were asked about their shopping habits.

Approximately when, if at all, was the last time you bought locally sourced produce for your household?

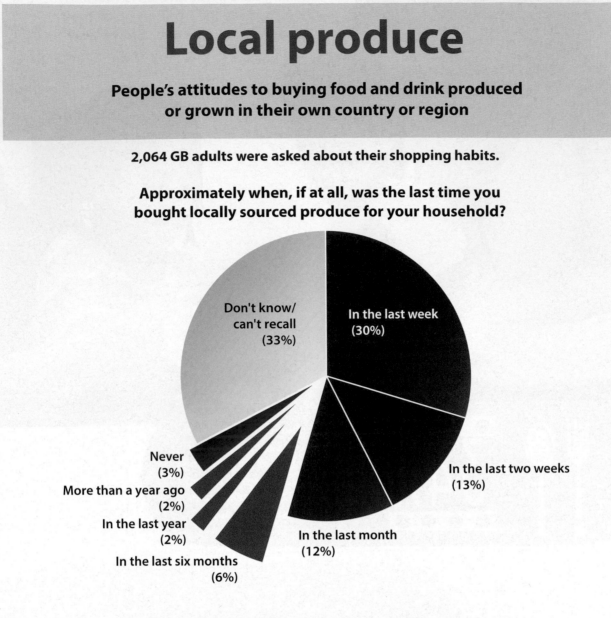

Don't know/ can't recall (33%)

In the last week (30%)

In the last two weeks (13%)

In the last month (12%)

In the last six months (6%)

In the last year (2%)

More than a year ago (2%)

Never (3%)

Which, if any of the following places would you generally expect to buy locally sourced produce from?
(more than one answer could be given)

77%
said a farm shop which sells produce from a farm directly to the public

38%
said a delicatessen selling cooked meat, cheeses etc

47%
said a supermarket

18%
said a convenience store
(a small shop stocking a limited range of household goods, foods, groceries etc)

2%
said none of these

4%
said they didn't know

Which TWO of the following would you be MOST likely to buy if a locally sourced alternative was available?

Vegetables	51%
Meat	40%
Eggs	30%
Milk	22%
Fruit	22%
Bread	12%
None of these	2%
Don't know	7%

Which, if any of the following do you think would ever PREVENT you from buying locally sourced produce
(more than one answer could be given)

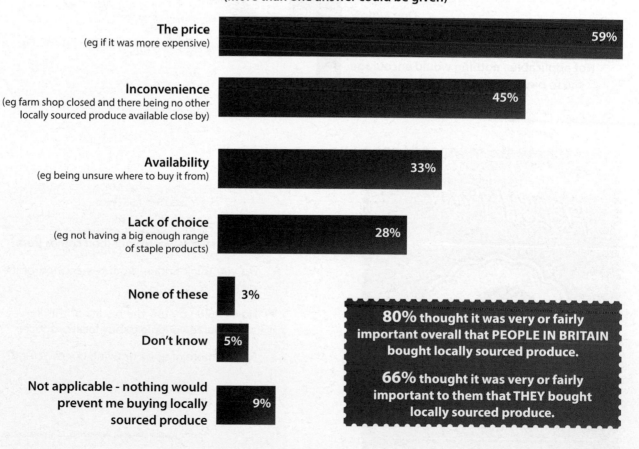

The price (eg if it was more expensive)	59%
Inconvenience (eg farm shop closed and there being no other locally sourced produce available close by)	45%
Availability (eg being unsure where to buy it from)	33%
Lack of choice (eg not having a big enough range of staple products)	28%
None of these	3%
Don't know	5%
Not applicable - nothing would prevent me buying locally sourced produce	9%

80% thought it was very or fairly important overall that PEOPLE IN BRITAIN bought locally sourced produce.

66% thought it was very or fairly important to them that THEY bought locally sourced produce.

Which, if any of the following do you think would ENCOURAGE you to buy more locally sourced produce

(more than one answer could be given)

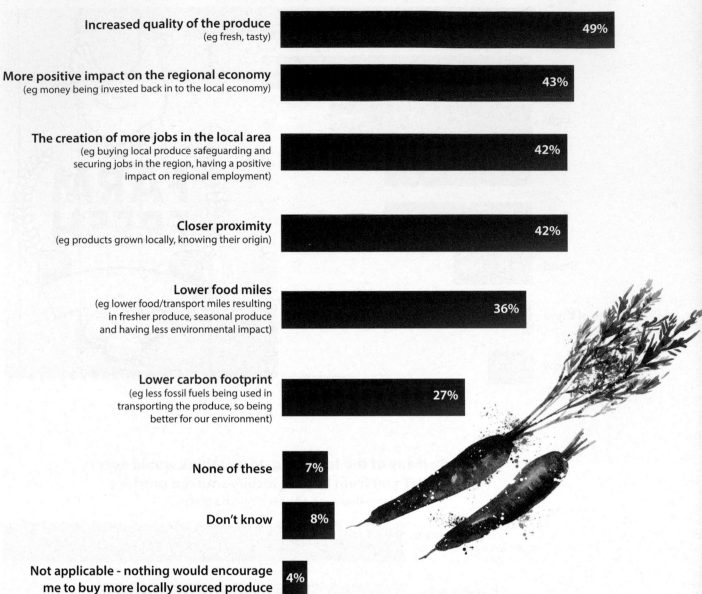

Increased quality of the produce
(eg fresh, tasty) — 49%

More positive impact on the regional economy
(eg money being invested back in to the local economy) — 43%

The creation of more jobs in the local area
(eg buying local produce safeguarding and securing jobs in the region, having a positive impact on regional employment) — 42%

Closer proximity
(eg products grown locally, knowing their origin) — 42%

Lower food miles
(eg lower food/transport miles resulting in fresher produce, seasonal produce and having less environmental impact) — 36%

Lower carbon footprint
(eg less fossil fuels being used in transporting the produce, so being better for our environment) — 27%

None of these — 7%

Don't know — 8%

Not applicable - nothing would encourage me to buy more locally sourced produce — 4%

FRESH Food!
LOCALLY GROWN

Watermelon

100% Natural

Some issues

- Does it matter where your food comes from?

- Do you think Britain produces enough of its own food?

- How could you use the results of this survey to encourage people to buy local produce?

- Should more of us be growing our own food?

Source: YouGov Omnibus Research 2015   yougov.co.uk

Food waste

We are wasting a lot of food, it affects the environment and our bank balance!

Food waste is a major issue. We throw away **7 million tonnes** of food and drink from our homes every year, the majority of which could have been eaten. It's costing us **£12.5bn** a year and is bad for the environment too.

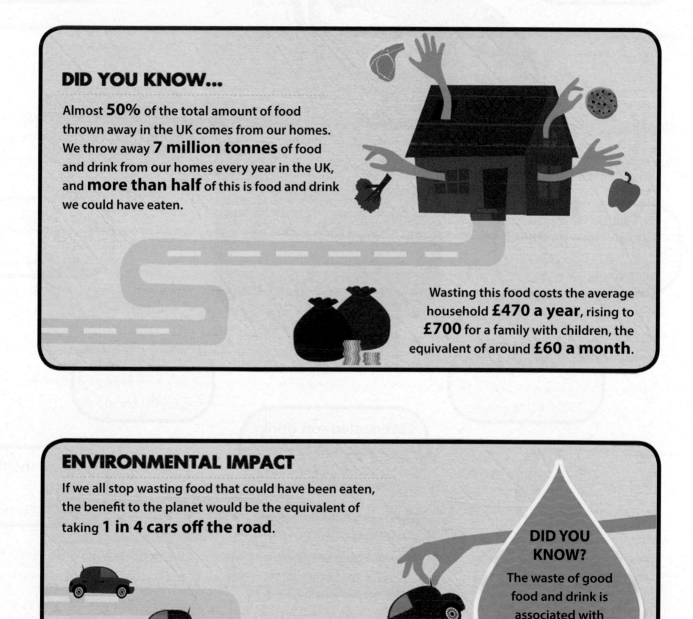

DID YOU KNOW...

Almost **50%** of the total amount of food thrown away in the UK comes from our homes. We throw away **7 million tonnes** of food and drink from our homes every year in the UK, and **more than half** of this is food and drink we could have eaten.

Wasting this food costs the average household **£470 a year**, rising to **£700** for a family with children, the equivalent of around **£60 a month**.

ENVIRONMENTAL IMPACT

If we all stop wasting food that could have been eaten, the benefit to the planet would be the equivalent of taking **1 in 4 cars off the road**.

DID YOU KNOW?

The waste of good food and drink is associated with **4%** of the UK's total **water footprint**.

What food do we waste?

Standard bread
£640,000,000
540,000 tonnes

Home made & pre-prepared meals
£1,700,000,000
490,000 tonnes

Wine
£480,000,000
51,000 tonnes

Poultry
£350,000,000
81,000 tonnes

Pork/ Ham/ Bacon
£440,000,000
93,000 tonnes

Speciality bread
£300,000,000
80,000 tonnes

Apples
£300,000,000
180,000 tonnes

Cakes/ gateau/ doughnuts/ pastries
£280,000,000
91,000 tonnes

Milk
£280,000,000
360,000 tonnes

Breakfast cereal
£210,000,000
75,000 tonnes

Cheese
£240,000,000
38,000 tonnes

Carbonated soft drinks
£250,000,000
280,000 tonnes

Beef
£240,000,000
43,000 tonnes

Fish & shellfish
£250,000,000
32,000 tonnes

Yoghurt/ yoghurt drink
£210,000,000
80,000 tonnes

Potatoes
£230,000,000
290,000 tonnes

Stone fruit
£170,000,000
43,000 tonnes

Savoury products
£180,000,000
45,000 tonnes

Condiments etc
£190,000,000
66,000 tonnes

Fruit juices & smoothies
£190,000,000
16,000 tonnes

WHY IS IT WASTED?

There are **two main reasons** why we throw away good food: we cook or prepare too much or we don't use it in time.

The foods we **waste the most** are fresh vegetables and salad, drinks, fresh fruit, and bakery items such as bread and cakes.

DID YOU KNOW?

We throw away more food from our homes than packaging in the UK every year.

Each month, the average family throws away almost **£60** of good food that was bought but not eaten, yet **57%** of us claim not to waste food (or very little).

In fact as a nation we are throwing away millions of tonnes of food and drink from our homes every year, and most of this could have been eaten.

And while **one in four** of us think that the food we throw away doesn't cost much, the fact is that food waste is hitting us in the pocket - it currently costs the typical household **£470 a year.**

Some issues

- Why do you think we are not concerned about wasting food?

- Why is it important to try to reduce the amount of food you waste?

- What can you do to reduce the food you waste?

Source: Love Food Hate Waste   www.lovefoodhatewaste.com

Health

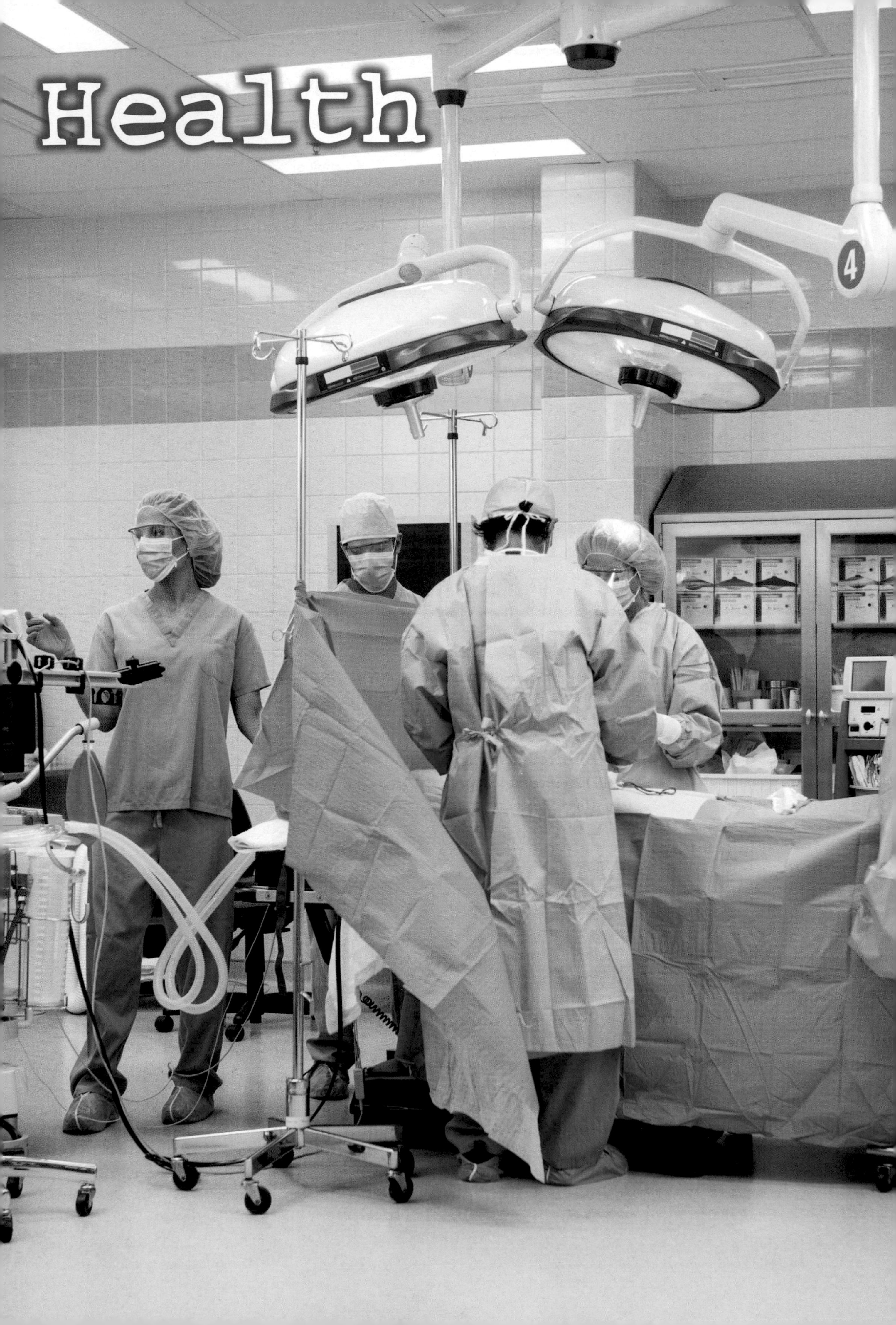

Satisfaction with the NHS

Public views and feelings towards NHS and health care issues

In 2014 a representative sample of 1,937 adults in England, Scotland and Wales were asked the NHS satisfaction question and a smaller sample of 971 were asked about their satisfaction with other NHS services.

Satisfaction with the NHS 1995 to 2014

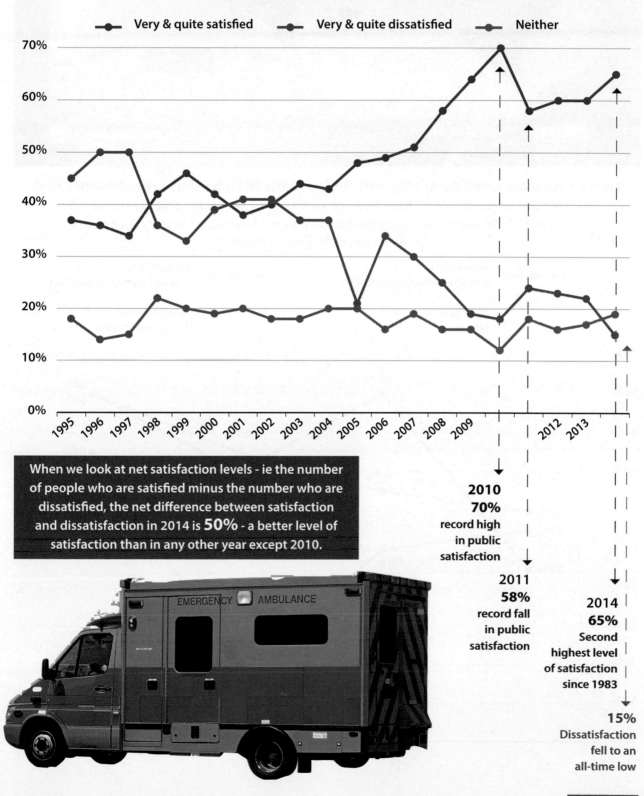

Legend: Very & quite satisfied — Very & quite dissatisfied — Neither

When we look at net satisfaction levels - ie the number of people who are satisfied minus the number who are dissatisfied, the net difference between satisfaction and dissatisfaction in 2014 is **50%** - a better level of satisfaction than in any other year except 2010.

2010
70%
record high in public satisfaction

2011
58%
record fall in public satisfaction

2014
65%
Second highest level of satisfaction since 1983

15%
Dissatisfaction fell to an all-time low

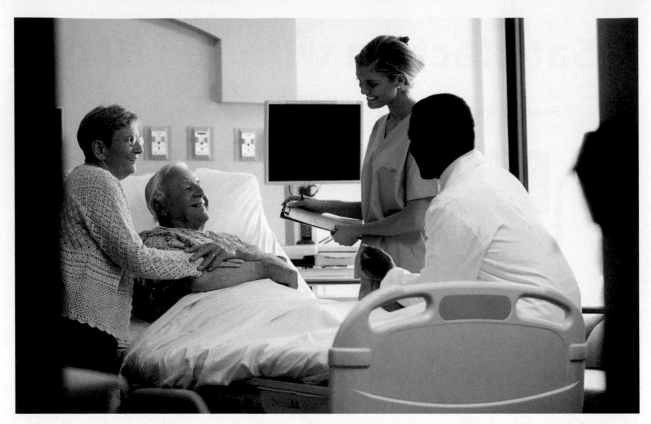

Those who were satisfied or very satisfied with the NHS, by those respondents who HAD recent experience of inpatient or outpatient services, and by those who HAD NOT had recent contact personally or by friends or family members

(Recent means in the past 12 months)

Inpatients
Recent personal contact

Outpatients
Recent personal contact

Inpatients
No recent contact

Outpatients
No recent contact

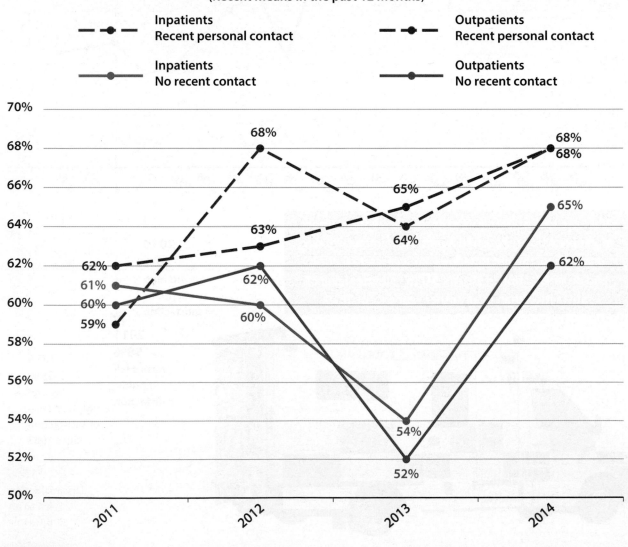

Satisfaction with social care services is considerably lower than for NHS services. Many people were less certain about their views on social care. This may be because they know less about these services and because there has been less media attention on them.

Satisfaction with social care compared to NHS services, 2014

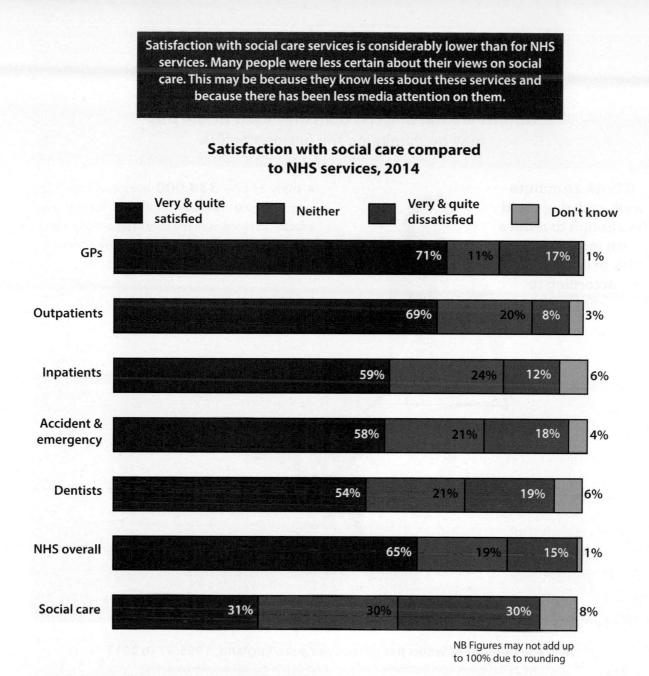

	Very & quite satisfied	Neither	Very & quite dissatisfied	Don't know
GPs	71%	11%	17%	1%
Outpatients	69%	20%	8%	3%
Inpatients	59%	24%	12%	6%
Accident & emergency	58%	21%	18%	4%
Dentists	54%	21%	19%	6%
NHS overall	65%	19%	15%	1%
Social care	31%	30%	30%	8%

NB Figures may not add up to 100% due to rounding

What do we mean by 'satisfaction'?

The increase in the public's level of satisfaction with the NHS between 2013 and 2014 might show that the public feel the health service improved in 2014.

However:

- NHS funding has been under increasing pressure since 2010 and performance problems with A&E waiting times and the 18-week maximum wait from referral to treatment have been featured in the media;

- In the results of monthly surveys, the public now lists the NHS as one of the top three issues facing Britain today.

The increase in satisfaction during a year in which the service was under pressure may reflect an actual increase but also a desire among the public to show support for the health service.

Some issues

- What is your own experience of NHS care?

- Why would people who have had recent contact with the NHS be more satisfied than those who hadn't?

- One measure of NHS success is how long people have to wait for A&E treatment. What would you do to improve waiting times?

- Should some types of patient have to pay for their care?

Source: The Kings Fund
www.kingsfund.org.uk/projects/bsa-survey-2014
NatCen Social Research's British Social Attitudes survey
www.natcen.ac.uk/our-research/research/british-social-attitudes

Walking for health

Britons are walking less than they used to and this may be damaging the nation's health

A brisk 20 minute walk each day could be enough to reduce an individual's risk of early death, according to research.

A study of over **334,000** European men and women found that lack of physical activity was a factor in twice as many deaths as obesity - and that just a modest increase in physical activity could have significant health benefits.

But people in Britain are walking less than they used to.

Average number of walks per person per year, England, 1995/97 to 2013

(**NB** 2001 is absent from the time line because of a change in the way data was presented)

1995/97	1998/00	2002	2003	2004	2005	2006	2007	2008	2009	2010	2011	2012	2013
292	269	241	245	249	247	250	218	220	228	213	220	212	203

Percentage of adults who walk for 20 minutes or more, by age, England, 2013

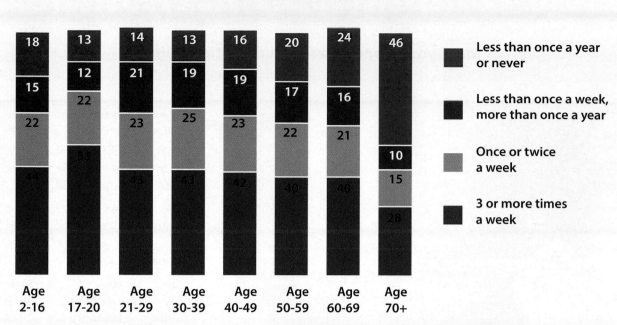

	Age 2-16	Age 17-20	Age 21-29	Age 30-39	Age 40-49	Age 50-59	Age 60-69	Age 70+
Less than once a year or never	18	13	14	13	16	20	24	46
Less than once a week, more than once a year	15	12	21	19	19	17	16	10
Once or twice a week	22	22	23	25	23	22	21	15
3 or more times a week	44	53	43	43	42	40	40	28

Percentage of all adults who walk for 20 minutes or more, England, 2013

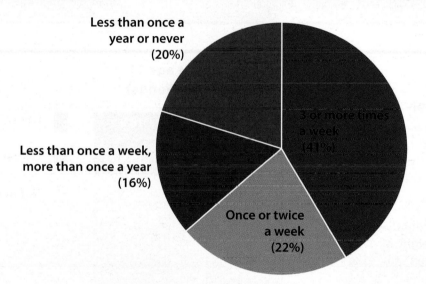

Less than once a year or never (20%)

Less than once a week, more than once a year (16%)

Once or twice a week (22%)

3 or more times a week (41%)

NB Figures do not add up to 100% due to rounding

Some issues

- Why is walking important for people's health?

- What do you think has influenced the decline in walking?

- How could people be encouraged to walk more?

Source: National Travel Survey , Department for Transport
© Crown copyright 2014 www.gov.uk
MRC Epidemiology Unit www.mrc-epid.cam.ac.uk/blog/
lack-exercise-premature-deaths

Overweight young people

More young people are an unhealthy weight

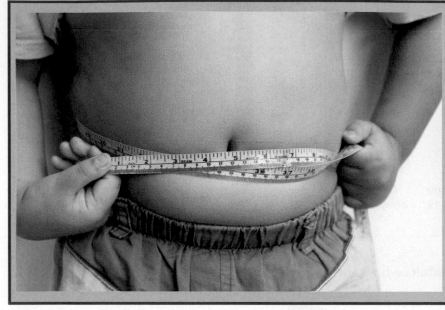

The Millennium Cohort Study follows the lives of a sample of about **19,000** babies born in the UK between September 2000 and January 2002.

The children were surveyed when they were 9 months old and again when they were aged 3, 5, 7 and 11.

The survey of 11-year-olds in January 2012 and February 2013 also reviewed how levels of overweight and obesity among the children had changed since earlier surveys.

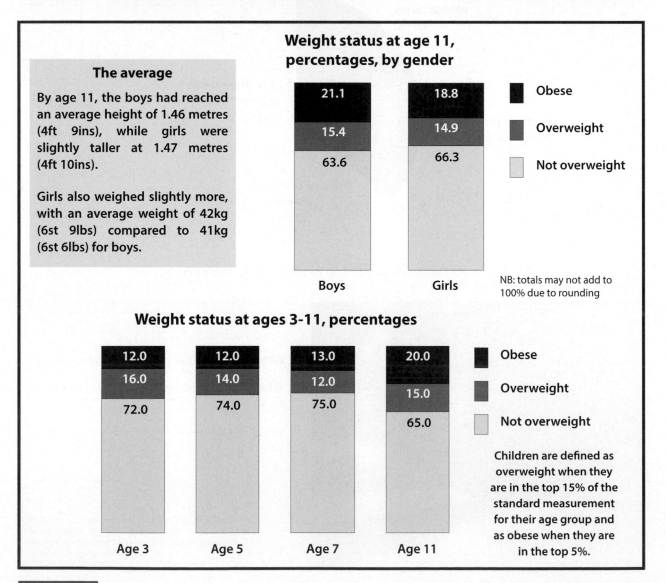

The average

By age 11, the boys had reached an average height of 1.46 metres (4ft 9ins), while girls were slightly taller at 1.47 metres (4ft 10ins).

Girls also weighed slightly more, with an average weight of 42kg (6st 9lbs) compared to 41kg (6st 6lbs) for boys.

Weight status at age 11, percentages, by gender

Boys: Obese 21.1, Overweight 15.4, Not overweight 63.6

Girls: Obese 18.8, Overweight 14.9, Not overweight 66.3

Legend: Obese, Overweight, Not overweight

NB: totals may not add to 100% due to rounding

Weight status at ages 3-11, percentages

Age 3: Obese 12.0, Overweight 16.0, Not overweight 72.0

Age 5: Obese 12.0, Overweight 14.0, Not overweight 74.0

Age 7: Obese 13.0, Overweight 12.0, Not overweight 75.0

Age 11: Obese 20.0, Overweight 15.0, Not overweight 65.0

Legend: Obese, Overweight, Not overweight

Children are defined as overweight when they are in the top 15% of the standard measurement for their age group and as obese when they are in the top 5%.

The Millennium Cohort Study could not look at older age groups but another study used electronic health records from the practices of 375 doctors to look at overweight and obesity in children in England and compare trends over two decades.

The final data analysed **370,544** children aged 2-15 years and a total of **507,483** BMI records.

Percentage, of children aged 11-15 whose measurements showed they were overweight (including obese)

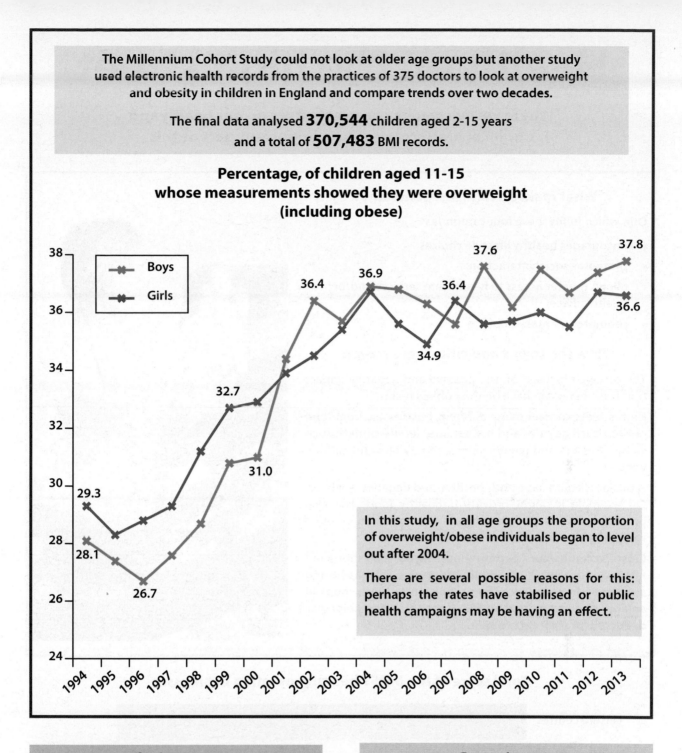

- Boys
- Girls

28.1
29.3
26.7
32.7
31.0
36.4
36.9
34.9
36.4
37.6
37.8
36.6

1994 1995 1996 1997 1998 1999 2000 2001 2002 2003 2004 2005 2006 2007 2008 2009 2010 2011 2012 2013

In this study, in all age groups the proportion of overweight/obese individuals began to level out after 2004.

There are several possible reasons for this: perhaps the rates have stabilised or public health campaigns may be having an effect.

Why it matters

Children who are overweight or obese face an increased risk of many health problems, including asthma, heart disease and type 2 diabetes. Childhood overweight and obesity is also associated with low self-esteem and depression, and can have a long lasting impact on an individual's life.

Some issues

- Do you agree that we should be concerned about the weight of young people?

- If children of 11 are overweight or obese, who should take responsibility for their health?

- What can be done by society in general to improve the situation?

- Do the different methods used for these two studies give a true picture?

Source: Child overweight and obesity Initial findings from the Millennium Cohort Study Age 11 Survey www.cls.ioe.ac.uk Childhood obesity trends from primary care electronic health records in England between 1994 and 2013: population-based cohort study, http://adc.bmj.com/content/100/3/214.full

Health on the high street

Where we live can have a great effect on our health and our local high streets are an important part of this

What makes a high street healthy?

One which fulfils these four categories:

- encourages healthy lifestyle choices;
- promotes social interaction;
- allows greater access to health care services and/or health advice;
- promotes mental wellbeing.

How the towns and cities were scored

The research focused on the positive and negative impact that businesses can have on the public's health.

High streets contain many different businesses, from food outlets, such as cafes and restaurants, service outlets, such as hairdressers and beauty salons, to retailers and cultural venues.

A business could have both positive and negative qualities. For example it might provide unhealthy foods but also provide a place for people to meet - which promotes mental wellbeing.

Clusters of pubs/bars, betting shops, payday loan shops and fast food takeaways on a high street were seen as having a negative impact. Once the proportion of these shops in an area came to more than 5% of the total, one point was deducted for each extra outlet.

Total score of the MOST health promoting businesses

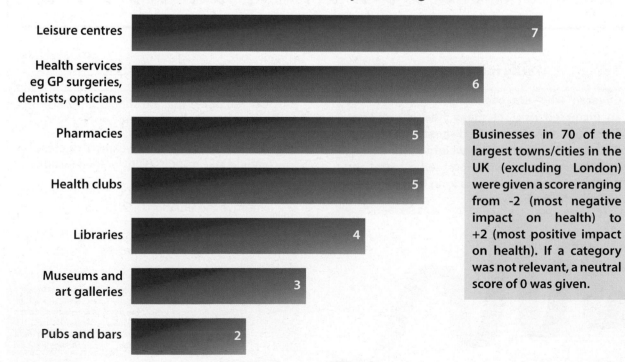

Business	Score
Leisure centres	7
Health services eg GP surgeries, dentists, opticians	6
Pharmacies	5
Health clubs	5
Libraries	4
Museums and art galleries	3
Pubs and bars	2

Businesses in 70 of the largest towns/cities in the UK (excluding London) were given a score ranging from -2 (most negative impact on health) to +2 (most positive impact on health). If a category was not relevant, a neutral score of 0 was given.

Pubs and bars

59% of people believe pubs/bars **discourage healthy choices**, however **75%** think they **support social interaction**.

33% say they have a **positive effect** on **mental wellbeing**.

Libraries

52% think libraries **support social interaction**.

66% believe they **support mental wellbeing**.

Health clubs

78% believe health clubs **support healthy choices**.

68% say they **promote social interaction**.

56% say they **support** access to **health services and advice**.

66% say they **support mental wellbeing**.

Top ten UK towns with the healthiest high streets

1	Shrewsbury
2	Ayr
3	Salisbury
4	Perth
5	Hereford
6	Carlisle
7	Cambridge
8	Cheltenham
9	York
10	Bristol

Healthiest high streets:
York 9th place

Total score of the LEAST health promoting businesses

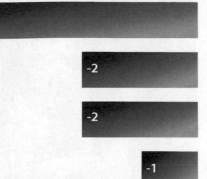

-4	Payday loan shops
-2	Bookmakers
-2	Fast food takeaways
-1	Tanning shops

Unhealthiest high streets:
Blackpool 4th place

Payday loans

Payday loan shops have become an increasingly common sight on our high streets with over 2,000 of them located across the UK.

68% of people think payday loan shops **discourage healthy choices.**

65% say they have a **negative impact** on **mental wellbeing.**

Fast food takeaways

69% think fast food takeaways **discourage healthy choices.**

52% say that they have a **negative impact** on **mental wellbeing.**

Tanning shops

62% believe they **discourage healthy choices.**

Top ten UK towns with the unhealthiest high streets

1	Preston
2	Middlesbrough
3	Coventry
4	Blackpool
5	Northampton
6	Wolverhampton
7	Grimsby
8	Huddersfield
9	Stoke-On-Trent
10	Eastbourne

Some issues

- Does it matter what shops and businesses are on our high streets?

- What else would improve the look of our towns and the health of people?

- What would your ideal high street look like?

Base: 2,000 members of the public were asked whether they thought certain businesses helped or hindered their health.

Source: Royal Society for Public Health - Health on the High Street, 2015
www.rsph.org.uk

Blood donors

Exotic travel, tattoos and medical investigations are some of the reasons for the decline in blood being donated

Blood stock levels in units 2005 to 2015

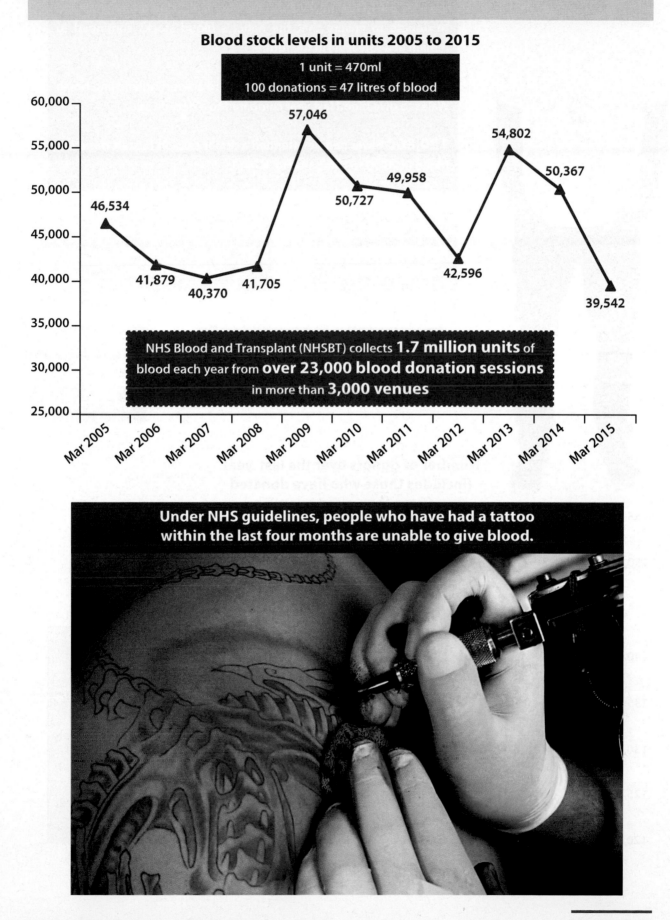

> 1 unit = 470ml
> 100 donations = 47 litres of blood

- Mar 2005: 46,534
- Mar 2006: 41,879
- Mar 2007: 40,370
- Mar 2008: 41,705
- Mar 2009: 57,046
- Mar 2010: 50,727
- Mar 2011: 49,958
- Mar 2012: 42,596
- Mar 2013: 54,802
- Mar 2014: 50,367
- Mar 2015: 39,542

> NHS Blood and Transplant (NHSBT) collects **1.7 million units** of blood each year from **over 23,000 blood donation sessions** in more than **3,000 venues**

Under NHS guidelines, people who have had a tattoo within the last four months are unable to give blood.

Only 4% of adults are active blood donors

New donors are needed to fill the gaps left by existing donors who are not able to give blood at this time and to ensure that there is the right mix of blood groups to match patients' needs

In 2015, **204,000** new volunteers were needed to attend a session to donate to ensure that the nation's blood stocks continued to remain at a safe level in the future.

40% fewer new volunteers came forward across England and North Wales to give blood last year compared to a decade ago.

120,000 fewer people attended a donor session to start donating blood in 2014/15 compared to 2004/5.

8% of donors are donating for the first time

Over 25% of us require blood at least once in our lifetime

January is the busiest month for donors honouring new year's resolutions

Each blood donation can help as many as 3 people

Number of donors over the last year (includes those who have donated more than once a year)

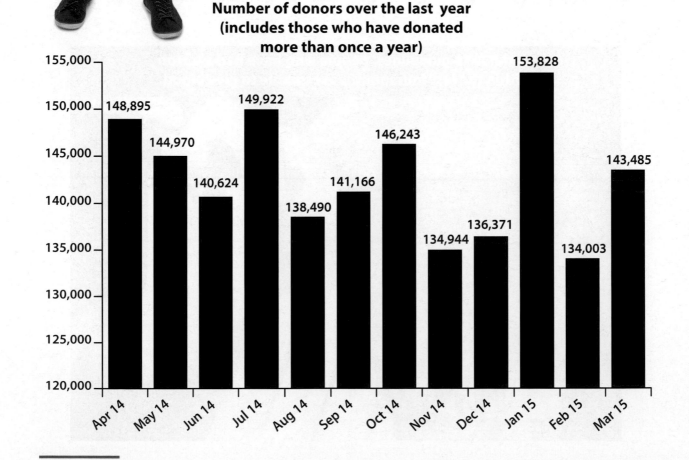

Some misunderstandings about donating blood.

A survey by NHS Blood and Transplant showed:

- **48%** thought that the NHS asked friends and family to donate when a patient needed blood;

- **13%** thought that synthetic blood was created to meet the national demand;

- Many people wrongly thought that a tattoo made them ineligible as donors for life.

BUT 80% of people knew that unpaid volunteers were the way that blood stocks are maintained.

Reasons why people don't give blood

The top three were:

- a fear of needles - **22%**;

- knowing it's a good thing to do but not getting around to it - **27%**;

- health problems (where they don't believe they are eligible to donate, which may not be the case) - **21%**.

BUT 86% of respondents who had given blood felt that it was as expected, or easier than they expected it to be.

56% said it made them feel worthwhile donating blood.

27% felt like they are giving something back to society.

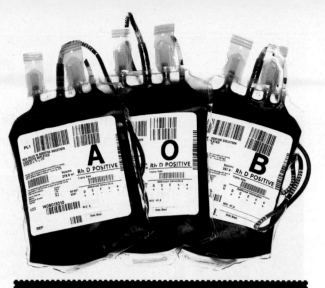

46% of English adults know their blood type.

34% of English adults who know their type, only did so after they donated blood for the first time.

Young UK adults aged 18-24 are the least likely age group to know their blood group with only **24%** knowing it.

Useful information:

If you are 17 or over you can find out if you are eligible to donate, register as a blood donor and book your appointment by contacting the NHSBT.

NHSBT's donor line: 0300 123 23 23
(24 hours a day, 7 days a week)
Website: www.blood.co.uk
Facebook: www.facebook.com/NHSBlood
Instagram @GivebloodNHS
Youtube: www.youtube.com/user/
NHSGiveBlood

Every year on 14th June, countries around the world celebrate **World Blood Donor Day** which raises awareness of the need for **safe** blood and thanks blood donors for their life-saving gifts of blood.

10% more blood is collected on **World Blood Donor Day** than any other day in June.

Some issues

- In some countries people are paid to donate their blood. Is this a good idea?

- What strategies would you suggest to get more people to give blood?

- What would persuade you, personally, to donate blood and what would prevent you?

Populus survey of 2,012 UK adults, May 2015

Source: NHSBT www.blood.co.uk
Populus www.populus.co.uk

Organ donation

The number of people who donated organs has fallen for the first time in 11 years

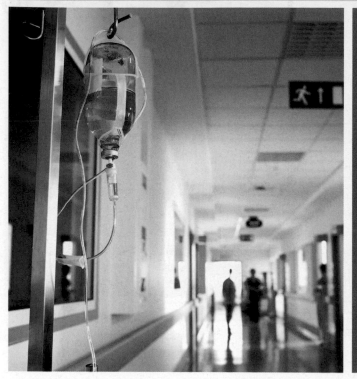

In 2014/15 **4,431** people in the UK had their lives saved or improved by an organ transplant but the number of people donating organs has fallen.

As well as **6,943** patients waiting for a transplant at the end of March 2015, a further **3,375** were temporarily suspended from transplant lists for reasons of health, fitness or availability.

429 patients died while on the active waiting list for their transplant and a further **807** were removed from the transplant list. This was usually because the patients' health had already deteriorated so much that many of them would have died shortly afterwards.

Number of donors, transplants and people waiting on the transplant list, 2005-2015

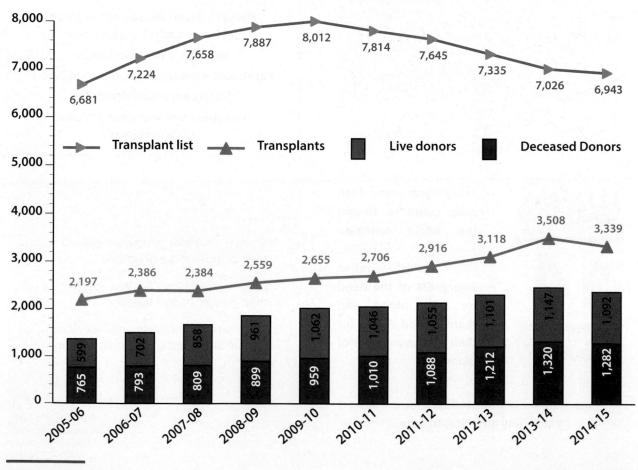

Transplant list: 6,681 · 7,224 · 7,658 · 7,887 · 8,012 · 7,814 · 7,645 · 7,335 · 7,026 · 6,943

Transplants: 2,197 · 2,386 · 2,384 · 2,559 · 2,655 · 2,706 · 2,916 · 3,118 · 3,508 · 3,339

Live donors: 599 · 702 · 858 · 961 · 1,062 · 1,046 · 1,055 · 1,101 · 1,147 · 1,092

Deceased Donors: 765 · 793 · 809 · 899 · 959 · 1,010 · 1,088 · 1,212 · 1,320 · 1,282

Years: 2005-06 · 2006-07 · 2007-08 · 2008-09 · 2009-10 · 2010-11 · 2011-12 · 2012-13 · 2013-14 · 2014-15

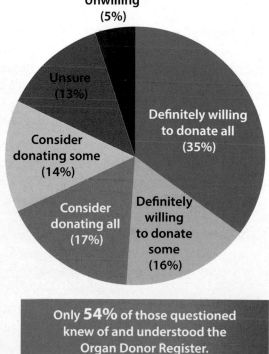

Some organs come from living donors, but in most cases organ transplantation is only possible because of the tragedy of a sudden and often premature death.

Fewer people died in circumstances where they could donate in 2014/15: **7,450** potential donors compared to **8,157** in 2013/14.

There is a strong support for organ donation

In a sample of 1,007 GB adults prepared by NHS Blood and Transplant, there was overwhelming support in principle for organ donation:

86%
supported it
(**50%** said they supported it 'strongly')

12%
were neutral; and

1%
said they didn't know

This left only
1%
opposed in principle
to organ donation.

Percentage saying whether they were personally willing to donate organs

Unwilling (5%)

Unsure (13%)

Consider donating some (14%)

Definitely willing to donate all (35%)

Consider donating all (17%)

Definitely willing to donate some (16%)

Only **54%** of those questioned knew of and understood the Organ Donor Register.
46% were either not aware of it or were not clear about what it did.

Top reasons why those who SUPPORT donation had NOT put their names on the Organ Donor Register

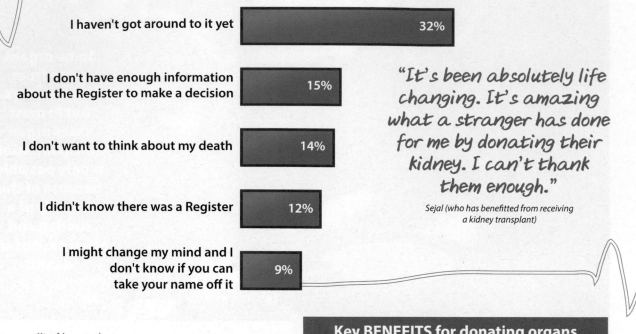

I haven't got around to it yet	32%
I don't have enough information about the Register to make a decision	15%
I don't want to think about my death	14%
I didn't know there was a Register	12%
I might change my mind and I don't know if you can take your name off it	9%

"It's been absolutely life changing. It's amazing what a stranger has done for me by donating their kidney. I can't thank them enough."

Sejal (who has benefitted from receiving a kidney transplant)

"What have you got to lose by signing up? If you end up a potential donor you won't need your organs. It is something positive for your loved ones to hold on to..."

Lloyd Dalton-Brown
(whose 29-year-old sister died after being hit by a truck and suffering fatal head injuries - her organs helped five people)

Key BENEFITS for donating organs

For those who would definitely donate their organs, the main reason was that they would be improving or saving the lives of others. Other reasons given were:

- that their organs would otherwise go to waste;
- it would feel good to help someone after death;
- someone you love could one day need a transplant; and
- if you are prepared to accept an organ you should be prepared to donate.

Key BARRIERS to donating organs

- a mistrust of medical professionals;
- a discomfort in thinking about death; and
- a lack of education about the donation process.

However, **39%** of people had no reservations about donation.

Bereaved families must be asked about whether organs can be donated.

The rate of consent for this was **58%.**

When a patient's wish to donate was known eg
- they were on the **NHS Organ Donor Register;**
- had talked about it with their family;
- had included their wishes in a Will etc,

the consent rate rose to **88.5%.**

The easiest way to make your agreement to organ donation known is to join the

Organ Donation Register
www.organdonation.nhs.uk
as **21 million** people have already done.

From December 2015, Wales will have an 'opt-out' system: It is assumed that you agree to your organs being used unless you have registered NOT to be a donor.

Some issues

- What can be done to increase the number of donors?
- Would you consider donating your organs after you have died?
- Should families discuss their wishes about organ donation?
- Which system is better, opt-in or opt-out?

Source: NHS Blood and Transplant www.nhsbt.nhs.uk
www.organdonation.nhs.uk   www.nhsbt.nhs.uk/life-stories

Internet
& media

Smartphones

Mobile communication is part of our everyday lives, bringing both benefits and pressures

46% of young people own a smartphone - **41%** use it daily.

Smartphones have widened young people's opportunities to access social media as they're always 'at hand'.

This encourages a continuous flow of communication and also allows for group chats.

It can be stressful to be 'always on'. The fact that a sender is notified when a message has been received and read can cause anxiety and misunderstandings in relationships with friends.

> *I think our generation has grown up to have a phone in its hand*
>
> *Girls, 14-15 age group, UK*

Photo posed by model

Socialising

Young people are used to feeling always connected, always able to get advice or news. They are able to manage their everyday life more conveniently and make use of 'dead' time.

For some young people though, this leads to them constantly searching, anxiously looking again and again just in case they have missed something.

> *I get so bored, sometimes I just pick it [smartphone] up and look at it and I have nothing.*
>
> *Or I'll go onto Instagram, come out of it, go on Twitter, come out of it, go on Snapchat and come out of it and just keep doing the circuit and I'll not realise I'm doing it...*
>
> *Girl, 14-16 age group, UK*

Daily use of smartphones, by country

Denmark **72%**

UK **56%**

Italy **42%**

Average **41%**

Portugal **35%**

Ireland **35%**

Belgium **28%**

Romania **21%**

Danish children were younger than children in the other countries surveyed when they were given their first mobile or smartphone - in contrast, Belgian children were older.

It's smaller so you always have it with you... if the possibility is there, you'll just use it more

Boy 15-16 age group, Belgium

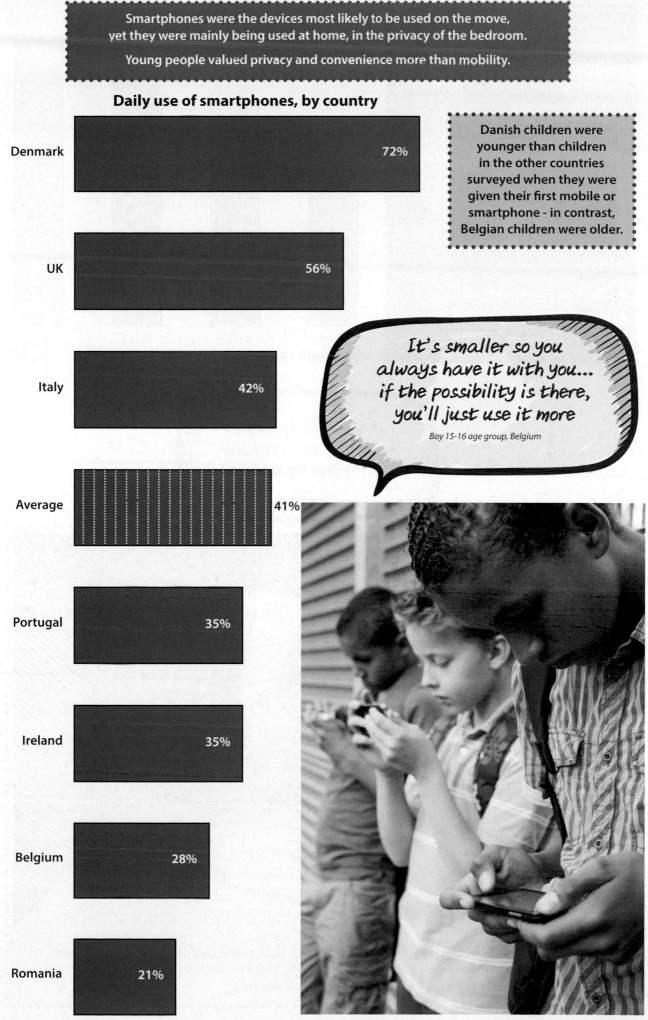

Photo posed by models

Age

After 2011 young people of all age groups were **more likely** to be given a **smartphone** than an **ordinary mobile** phone.

15% of those surveyed had never owned a mobile phone that was **not** a smartphone.

Daily use

13% of 9-10 year olds;

35% of 11-12 year olds;

52% of 13-14 year olds; and

60% of 15-16 year olds used a smartphone every day.

What age were you when you got your first smartphone?

9-10 years old	11-12 year old	13-14 year old	15-16 year old
8%	11%	12%	14%

...basically I always have the smartphone in my hand

Girl 15 Italy

Photo posed by model

Many young people agreed that they spent too much time online and/or on their smartphones. Smartphones are seen as extensions of their body, that can be easily stored in a pocket and carried around all day long.

Excessive use of smartphones

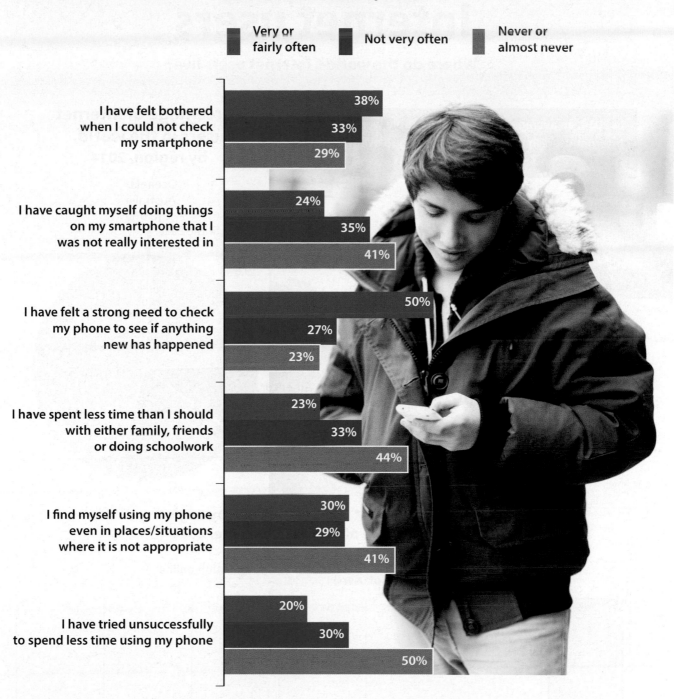

Legend:
- Very or fairly often
- Not very often
- Never or almost never

I have felt bothered when I could not check my smartphone
- 38%
- 33%
- 29%

I have caught myself doing things on my smartphone that I was not really interested in
- 24%
- 35%
- 41%

I have felt a strong need to check my phone to see if anything new has happened
- 50%
- 27%
- 23%

I have spent less time than I should with either family, friends or doing schoolwork
- 23%
- 33%
- 44%

I find myself using my phone even in places/situations where it is not appropriate
- 30%
- 29%
- 41%

I have tried unsuccessfully to spend less time using my phone
- 20%
- 30%
- 50%

The young people interviewed believed they were more 'sociable' since they had a smartphone:

" I talk more and I talk to a lot more people in general because the ability is there in my hands. "

Boy, UK

Some issues

- What do you think is an appropriate age for getting a smartphone?

- How would you define 'excessive' use of a smartphone?

- Should parents be checking how much young people use their smartphones?

- How do you think smartphones influence people's social skills?

Base: 3,500 young internet users, aged 9-16, in Belgium, Denmark, Ireland, Italy, Portugal, Romania and the UK.

Source: Net Children Go Mobile   www.netchildrengomobile.eu

Internet users

Where do the world's internet users live?

In 2014, an average of **42.3%** of people were internet users in the world, amounting to over **3 billion** users.

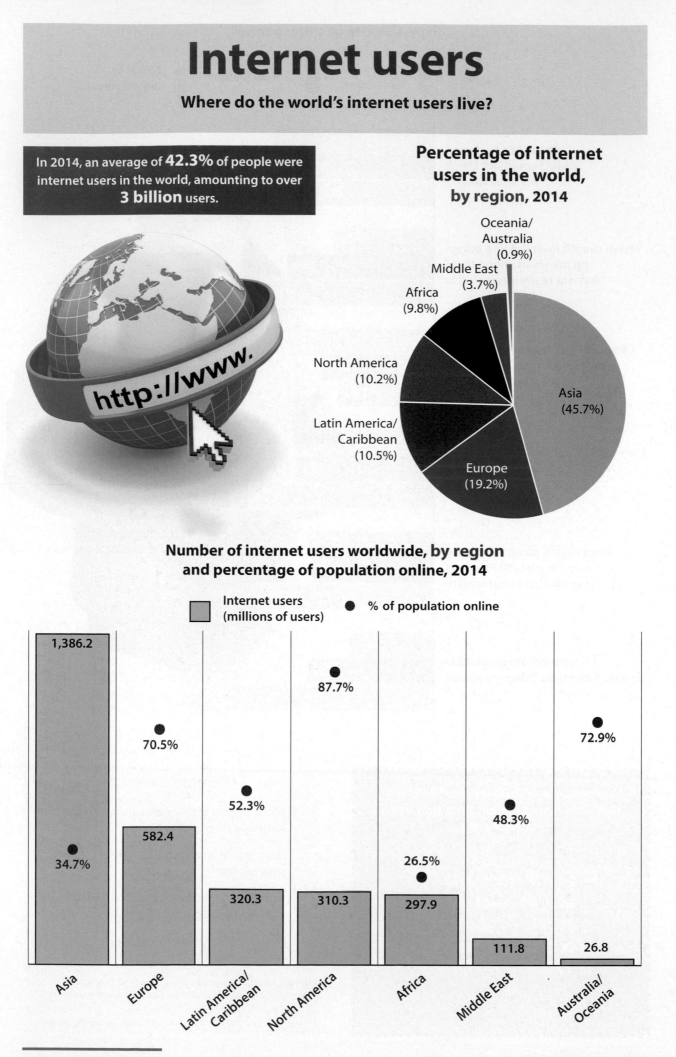

Percentage of internet users in the world, by region, 2014

- Oceania/Australia (0.9%)
- Middle East (3.7%)
- Africa (9.8%)
- North America (10.2%)
- Latin America/Caribbean (10.5%)
- Europe (19.2%)
- Asia (45.7%)

Number of internet users worldwide, by region and percentage of population online, 2014

- **Internet users (millions of users)**
- ● **% of population online**

Region	Internet users (millions)	% of population online
Asia	1,386.2	34.7%
Europe	582.4	70.5%
Latin America/Caribbean	320.3	52.3%
North America	310.3	87.7%
Africa	297.9	26.5%
Middle East	111.8	48.3%
Australia/Oceania	26.8	72.9%

Highest number of users (millions)
Top 20 countries
(latest available figures, 2013)

Country	Users (millions)
China	620.9
US	268.5
India	195.2
Brazil	109.7
Japan	109.6
Russia	87.5
Germany	69.8
Nigeria	67.3
UK	57.3
France	55.2
Indonesia	55.0
Mexico	52.3
Iran	45.0
Philippines	44.2
Egypt	43.1
Korea (South)	41.6
Vietnam	41.0
Turkey	37.7
Italy	36.1
Spain	35.7

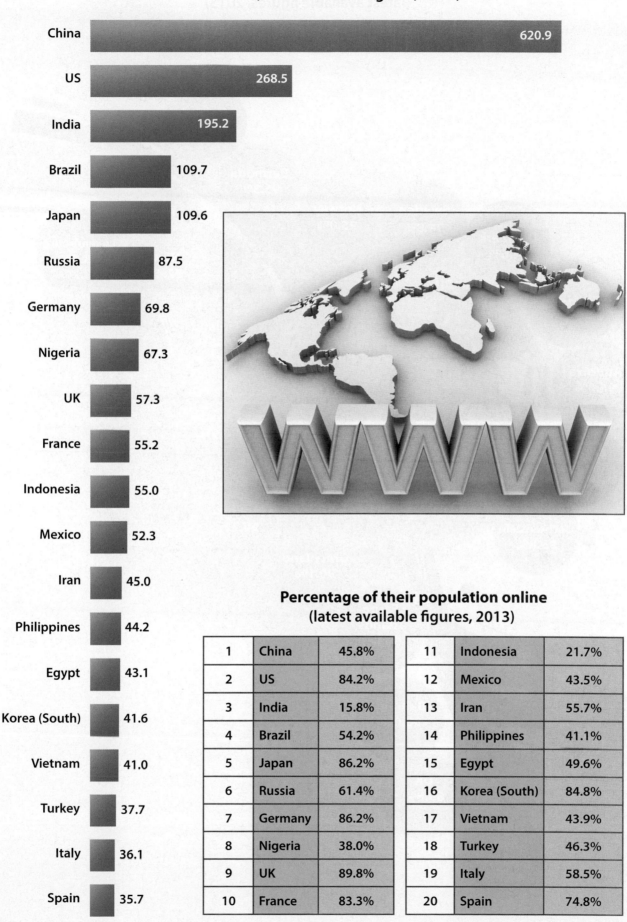

Percentage of their population online
(latest available figures, 2013)

#	Country	%	#	Country	%
1	China	45.8%	11	Indonesia	21.7%
2	US	84.2%	12	Mexico	43.5%
3	India	15.8%	13	Iran	55.7%
4	Brazil	54.2%	14	Philippines	41.1%
5	Japan	86.2%	15	Egypt	49.6%
6	Russia	61.4%	16	Korea (South)	84.8%
7	Germany	86.2%	17	Vietnam	43.9%
8	Nigeria	38.0%	18	Turkey	46.3%
9	UK	89.8%	19	Italy	58.5%
10	France	83.3%	20	Spain	74.8%

Highest percentage of their population online

Top 20 internet countries
(latest available figures, 2013)

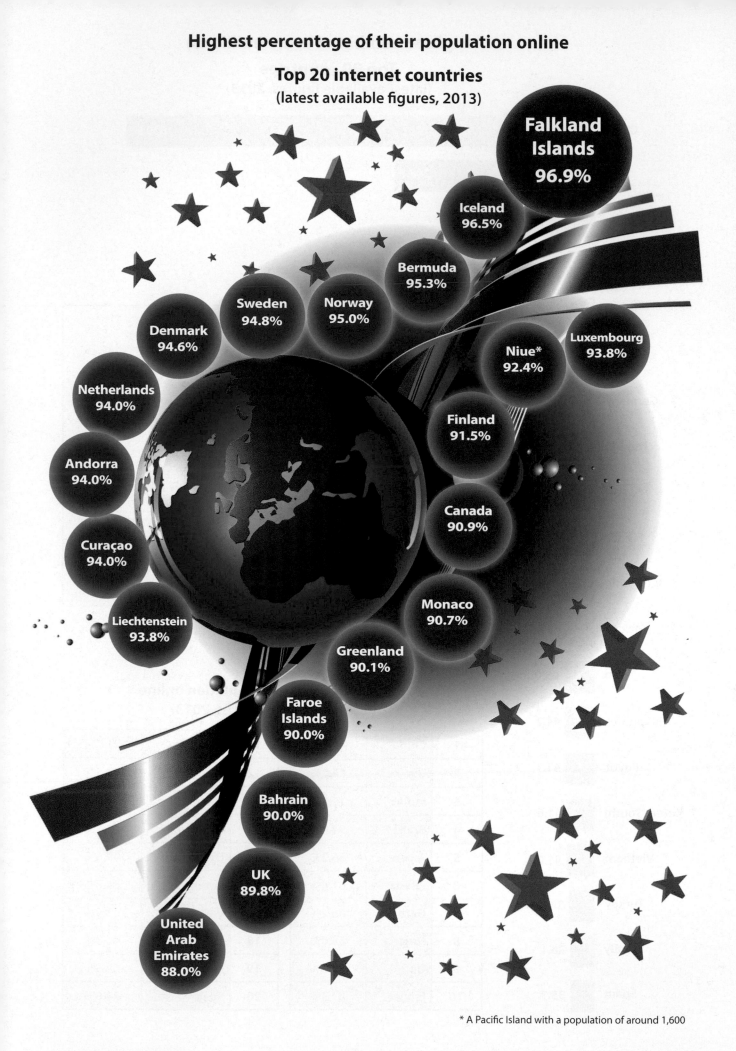

Falkland Islands 96.9%

Iceland 96.5%

Bermuda 95.3%

Norway 95.0%

Sweden 94.8%

Denmark 94.6%

Luxembourg 93.8%

Niue* 92.4%

Netherlands 94.0%

Finland 91.5%

Andorra 94.0%

Curaçao 94.0%

Canada 90.9%

Liechtenstein 93.8%

Monaco 90.7%

Greenland 90.1%

Faroe Islands 90.0%

Bahrain 90.0%

UK 89.8%

United Arab Emirates 88.0%

* A Pacific Island with a population of around 1,600

Top 10 EU28 internet countries
and % of their population online
(latest available figures, 2013)

Internet users
(millions of users)

● % of population online

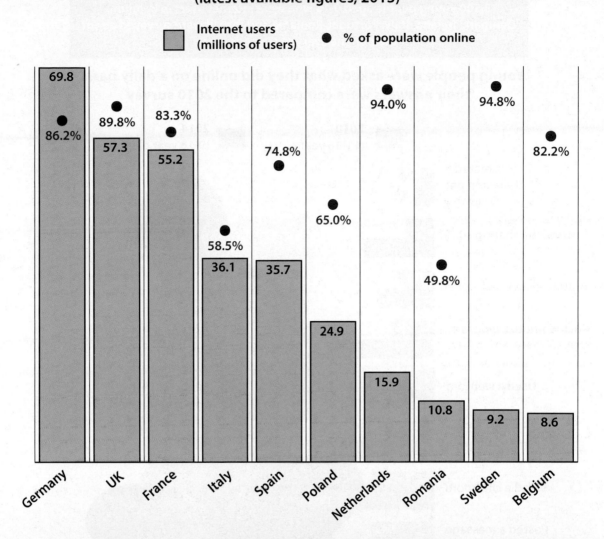

Country	Internet users (millions)	% of population online
Germany	69.8	86.2%
UK	57.3	89.8%
France	55.2	83.3%
Italy	36.1	58.5%
Spain	35.7	74.8%
Poland	24.9	65.0%
Netherlands	15.9	94.0%
Romania	10.8	49.8%
Sweden	9.2	94.8%
Belgium	8.6	82.2%

Some issues

- The countries with the highest number of users are different from the countries with the highest percentage of users. Can you suggest any reasons for this?

- Some of the top 20 countries by percentage of users might surprise you. Can you think what reasons there might be for high percentages in Luxembourg and in the Falkland Islands?

- What factors would boost the percentage of internet users in a country?

- Should countries with only a small percentage of internet users make a priority of expanding access? Or are other things more important?

- Should access to the internet be a human right like access to education?

Source: Internet World Stats   www.internetworldstats.com

EU kids online

Has the internet become any safer for young people?

3,500 young people aged 9-16 who were internet users in Belgium, Denmark, Ireland, Italy, Portugal, Romania and the UK were surveyed about their online everyday experiences.

Young people were asked what they did online on a daily basis - their answers were compared to the 2010 survey

2010 (11-16 year olds) **2014** (9-16 year olds)

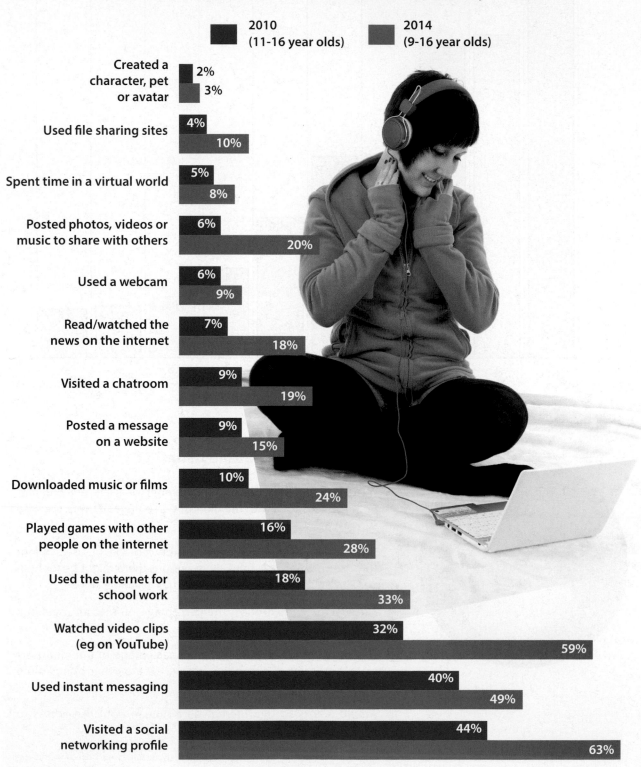

Activity	2010	2014
Created a character, pet or avatar	2%	3%
Used file sharing sites	4%	10%
Spent time in a virtual world	5%	8%
Posted photos, videos or music to share with others	6%	20%
Used a webcam	6%	9%
Read/watched the news on the internet	7%	18%
Visited a chatroom	9%	19%
Posted a message on a website	9%	15%
Downloaded music or films	10%	24%
Played games with other people on the internet	16%	28%
Used the internet for school work	18%	33%
Watched video clips (eg on YouTube)	32%	59%
Used instant messaging	40%	49%
Visited a social networking profile	44%	63%

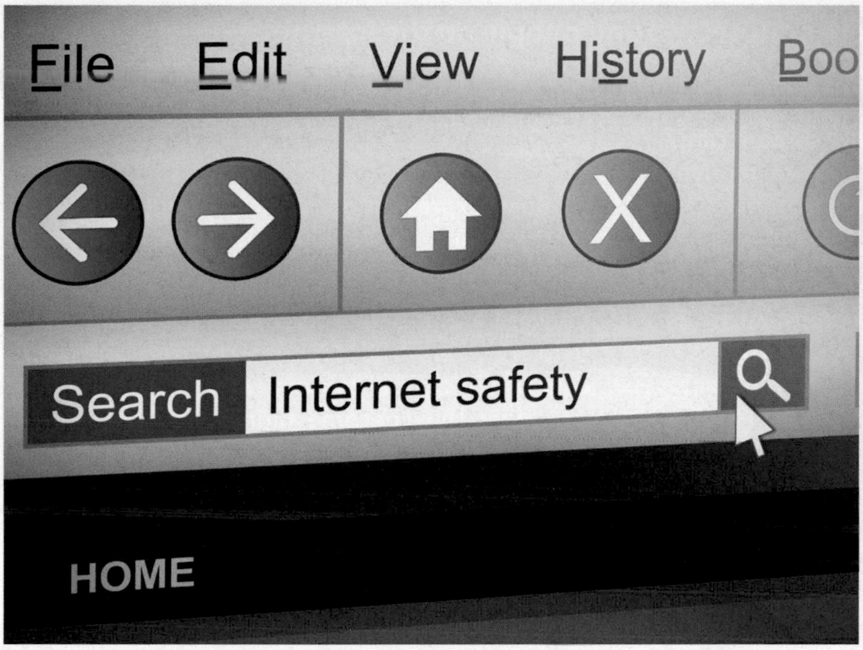

File Edit View History Boo

Search | Internet safety

HOME

Overall, **46%** of young people had experienced at **least one** risky situation on the internet. The most common risks overall were:

seeing sexual images online or offline
28%;

seeing potentially negative user generated content
25%;
and

being bullied online or offline
23%.

Compared to the 2010 survey, young people say they are now:

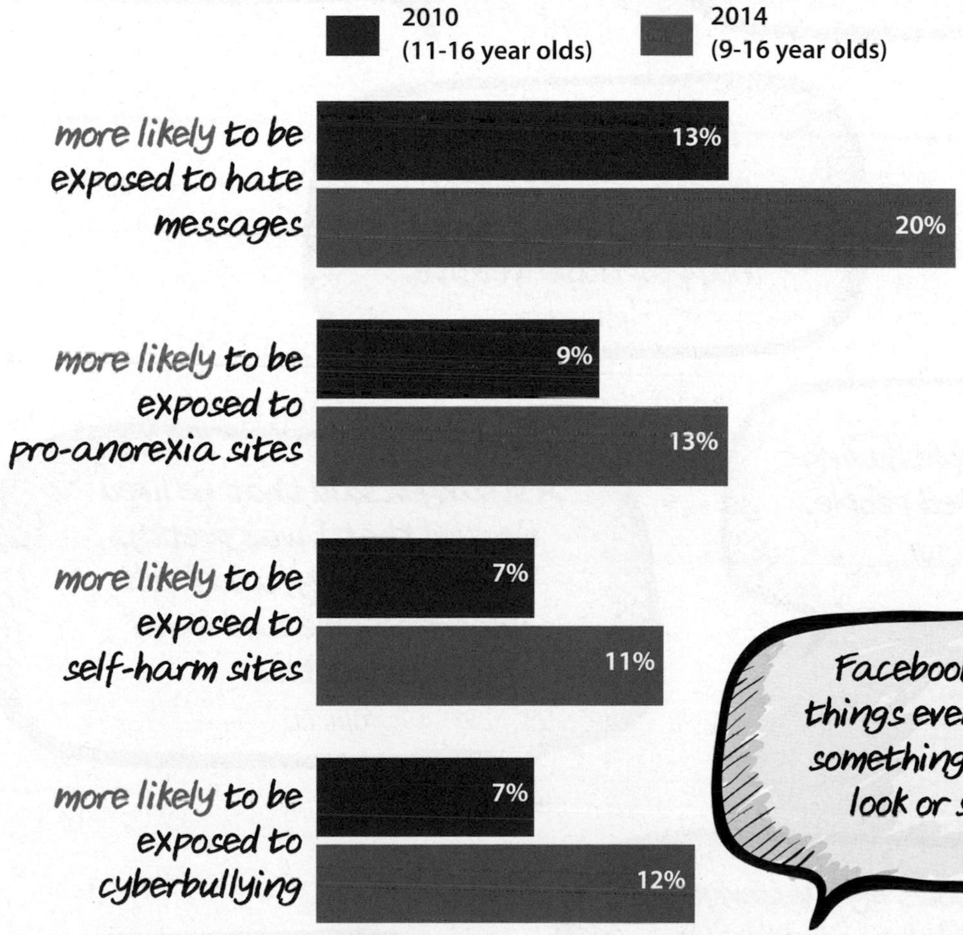

- ■ 2010 (11-16 year olds)
- ■ 2014 (9-16 year olds)

more likely to be exposed to hate messages
- 13%
- 20%

more likely to be exposed to pro-anorexia sites
- 9%
- 13%

more likely to be exposed to self-harm sites
- 7%
- 11%

more likely to be exposed to cyberbullying
- 7%
- 12%

> *Facebook shows scary things even if you click on something that does not look or sound scary.*
>
> *(Girl, 9)*

European 9 - 16 year olds are:

more likely to be upset by something seen online
- 13%
- 17%

What bothers or upsets young people on the internet?

- Pornography tops their online concerns.

- Violent, aggressive, cruel or gory content came a close second – although violence receives less public attention than sexual material.

- What particularly upsets them is real (or realistic) rather than fictional violence, and violence against the vulnerable such as children or animals.

- Video-sharing websites are seen as most linked with violent, pornographic and other content risks.

- Boys express more concern about violence than girls, while girls are more concerned about contact risks.

Concern about online risks rises noticeably from 9 to 12 years old. Younger children are more concerned about content risks, and as they get older they become more concerned about conduct and contact risks.

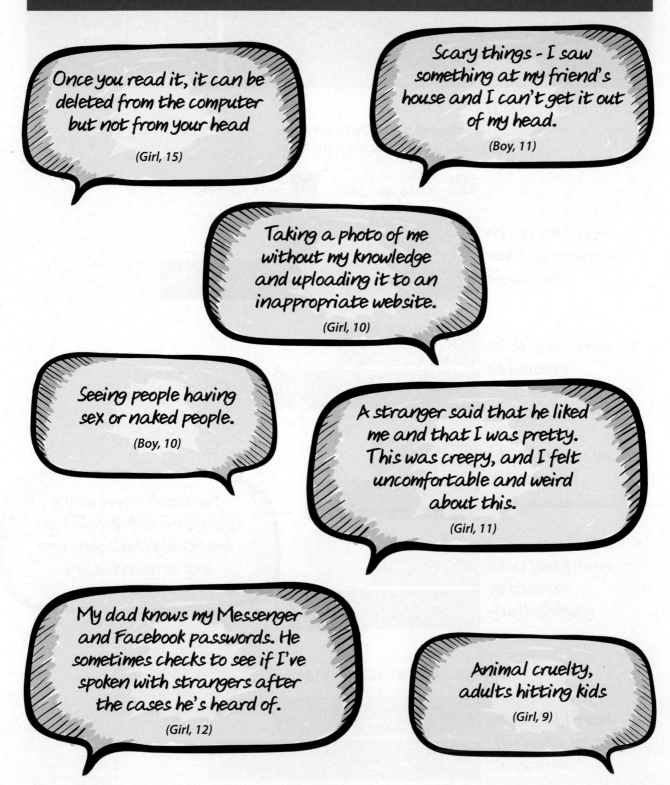

Once you read it, it can be deleted from the computer but not from your head

(Girl, 15)

Scary things - I saw something at my friend's house and I can't get it out of my head.

(Boy, 11)

Taking a photo of me without my knowledge and uploading it to an inappropriate website.

(Girl, 10)

Seeing people having sex or naked people.

(Boy, 10)

A stranger said that he liked me and that I was pretty. This was creepy, and I felt uncomfortable and weird about this.

(Girl, 11)

My dad knows my Messenger and Facebook passwords. He sometimes checks to see if I've spoken with strangers after the cases he's heard of.

(Girl, 12)

Animal cruelty, adults hitting kids

(Girl, 9)

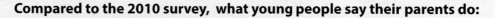

Are parents changing their approach to supporting their children's internet use? Not very much.

Compared to the 2010 survey, what young people say their parents do:

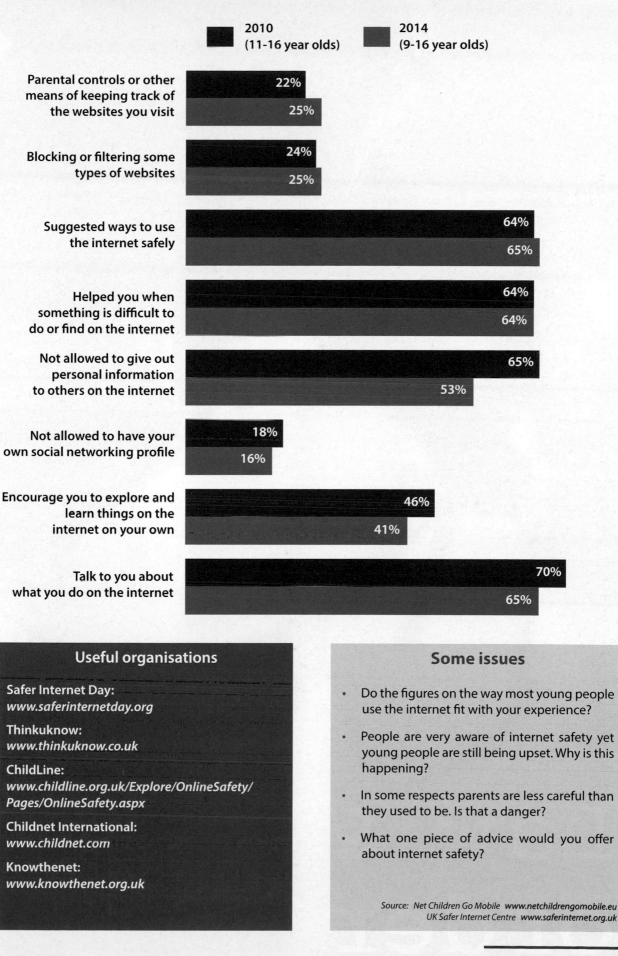

2010 (11-16 year olds)

2014 (9-16 year olds)

Parental controls or other means of keeping track of the websites you visit
- 22%
- 25%

Blocking or filtering some types of websites
- 24%
- 25%

Suggested ways to use the internet safely
- 64%
- 65%

Helped you when something is difficult to do or find on the internet
- 64%
- 64%

Not allowed to give out personal information to others on the internet
- 65%
- 53%

Not allowed to have your own social networking profile
- 18%
- 16%

Encourage you to explore and learn things on the internet on your own
- 46%
- 41%

Talk to you about what you do on the internet
- 70%
- 65%

Useful organisations

Safer Internet Day:
www.saferinternetday.org

Thinkuknow:
www.thinkuknow.co.uk

ChildLine:
www.childline.org.uk/Explore/OnlineSafety/Pages/OnlineSafety.aspx

Childnet International:
www.childnet.com

Knowthenet:
www.knowthenet.org.uk

Some issues

- Do the figures on the way most young people use the internet fit with your experience?

- People are very aware of internet safety yet young people are still being upset. Why is this happening?

- In some respects parents are less careful than they used to be. Is that a danger?

- What one piece of advice would you offer about internet safety?

Source: Net Children Go Mobile www.netchildrengomobile.eu
UK Safer Internet Centre www.saferinternet.org.uk

Law &
order

Prison overcrowding

75% of men's prisons in England and Wales are overcrowded

The prison population is rising and the number of prison places is falling

Certified Normal Accommodation (CNA) is the Prison Service's own measure of accommodation. It represents the good, decent standard of accommodation that the Service aspires to provide all prisoners.

The current CNA of the prison system, not counting cells that are out of use because of damage or building work is **75,196** people. The prison population in February 2015 was **84,121** meaning that on average, prisons were operating at **112%** of their capacity - and some prisons were much more crowded.

At its worst, overcrowding can mean two prisoners sharing a small cell designed for one with little ventilation and an unscreened toilet at the foot of the bunks.

Official inspections have found prisoners spending up to 23 hours a day in such conditions, as overcrowded prisons lack the resources to house people safely, give them something to do and reduce reoffending following release.

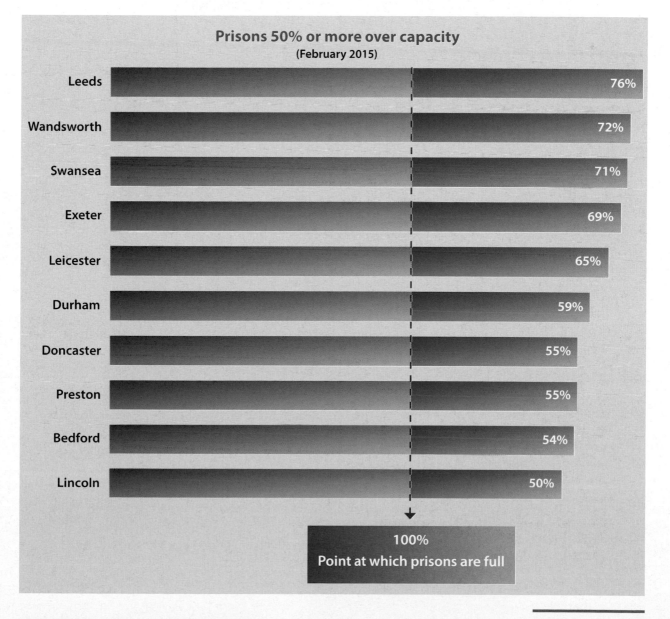

Prisons 50% or more over capacity
(February 2015)

Prison	% over capacity
Leeds	76%
Wandsworth	72%
Swansea	71%
Exeter	69%
Leicester	65%
Durham	59%
Doncaster	55%
Preston	55%
Bedford	54%
Lincoln	50%

100%
Point at which prisons are full

In 2013-14...

- The total cost of the prison service was **£2,832 million.**

- Each prisoner cost an average of **£33,785.**

"Caging men in squalor with nothing to do all day is never going to help them become law-abiding citizens on release."

Frances Crook, Chief Executive of the
Howard League for Penal Reform

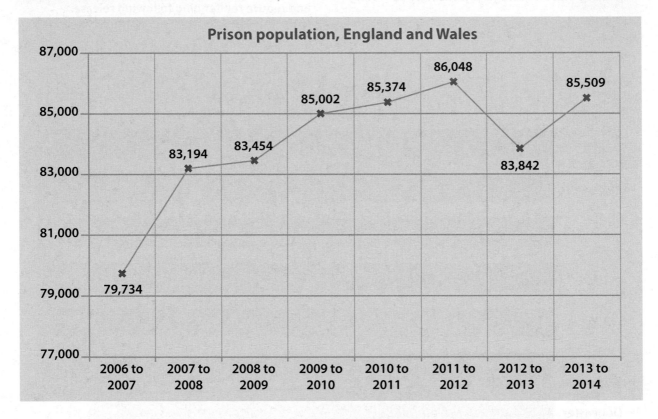

Prison population, England and Wales

Data points:
- 2006 to 2007: 79,734
- 2007 to 2008: 83,194
- 2008 to 2009: 83,454
- 2009 to 2010: 85,002
- 2010 to 2011: 85,374
- 2011 to 2012: 86,048
- 2012 to 2013: 83,842
- 2013 to 2014: 85,509

In 2013–14 on a typical day, almost **19,000** prisoners were **doubled-up**, meaning two prisoners were in a cell intended for one.

About **800** were **trebled-up** - three in a cell intended for two.

Factors contributing to the rise in prison population

- More people are being held in custody while awaiting trial (on remand).

- More people have been recalled to prison for breaking the terms of their release.

- Sentence length has increased.

- Those on set sentences have served more time before being released.

- The number serving very long or life sentences has increased.

The prison population will probably increase in the future

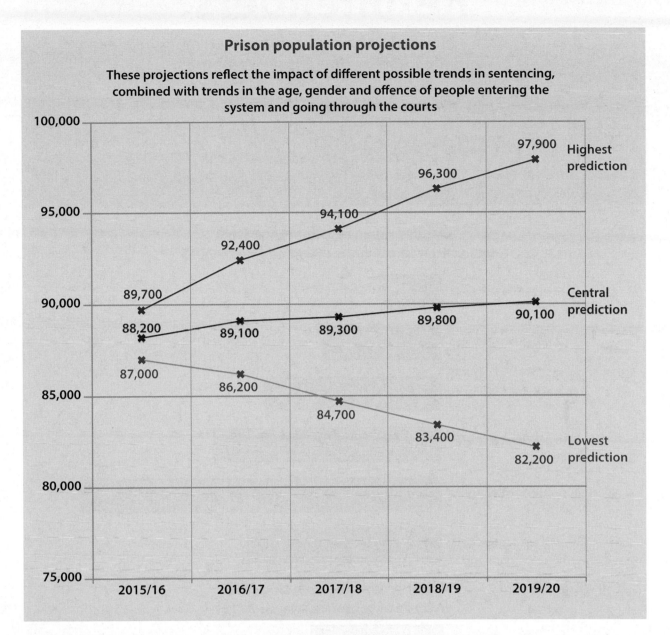

Prison population projections

These projections reflect the impact of different possible trends in sentencing, combined with trends in the age, gender and offence of people entering the system and going through the courts

Highest prediction
- 2015/16: 89,700
- 2016/17: 92,400
- 2017/18: 94,100
- 2018/19: 96,300
- 2019/20: 97,900

Central prediction
- 2015/16: 88,200
- 2016/17: 89,100
- 2017/18: 89,300
- 2018/19: 89,800
- 2019/20: 90,100

Lowest prediction
- 2015/16: 87,000
- 2016/17: 86,200
- 2017/18: 84,700
- 2018/19: 83,400
- 2019/20: 82,200

Some issues

- Does prison work as a punishment?

- Is prison an effective way to reform criminals?

- Are there more effective ways of reducing crime?

- Should the majority of people be concerned or pleased by the likelihood of a bigger prison population?

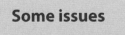

Source: Ministry of Justice © Crown copyright 2015
www.justice.gov.uk
Howard League for Penal Reform www.howardleague.org
Prison The Facts www.prisonreformtrust.org.uk

Re-offenders

About a quarter of people who have completed their punishment commit another crime within 12 months

Reoffenders are people who have been sentenced for an offence but go on to commit another one.

Around **485,000** adult offenders in England & Wales were cautioned, convicted or released from custody between April 2012 and March 2013.

Around **121,000** of them re-offended within a year - a rate of **25%**.

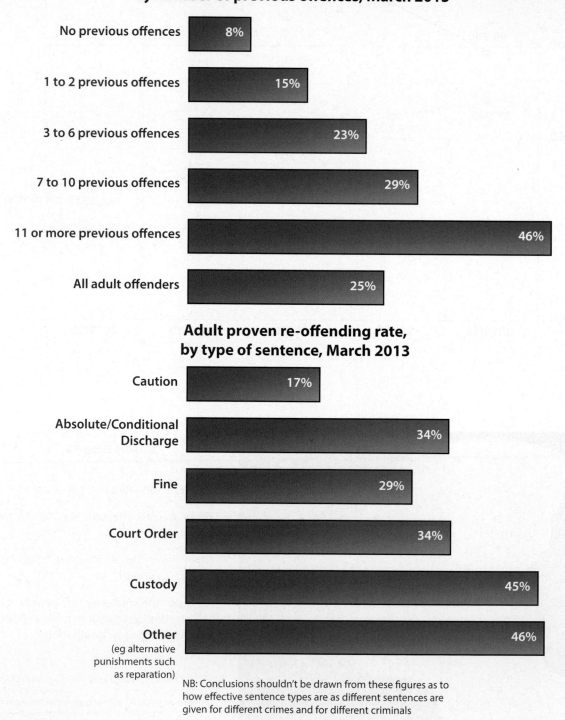

Adult proven re-offending rate by number of previous offences, March 2013

No previous offences	8%
1 to 2 previous offences	15%
3 to 6 previous offences	23%
7 to 10 previous offences	29%
11 or more previous offences	46%
All adult offenders	25%

Adult proven re-offending rate, by type of sentence, March 2013

Caution	17%
Absolute/Conditional Discharge	34%
Fine	29%
Court Order	34%
Custody	45%
Other (eg alternative punishments such as reparation)	46%

NB: Conclusions shouldn't be drawn from these figures as to how effective sentence types are as different sentences are given for different crimes and for different criminals

Percentage of adults re-offending within 12 months, ending March 2013, by original offence

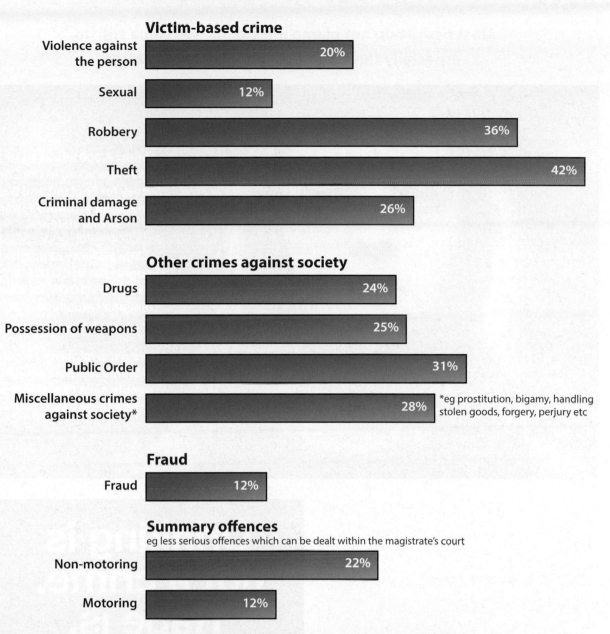

Victim-based crime

Offence	Percentage
Violence against the person	20%
Sexual	12%
Robbery	36%
Theft	42%
Criminal damage and Arson	26%

Other crimes against society

Offence	Percentage
Drugs	24%
Possession of weapons	25%
Public Order	31%
Miscellaneous crimes against society*	28%

*eg prostitution, bigamy, handling stolen goods, forgery, perjury etc

Fraud

Offence	Percentage
Fraud	12%

Summary offences
eg less serious offences which can be dealt within the magistrate's court

Offence	Percentage
Non-motoring	22%
Motoring	12%

The rate for other crimes not classified above is **26.8%**

NB All figures have been rounded

Some issues

- Does the re-offending rate prove that punishment isn't working?

- What should the prison system be doing to help ex-offenders to avoid re-offending?

- What conclusions would you draw from the figures about the original offence of the re-offenders?

- What would you do about the repeat re-offenders?

Source: Ministry of Justice © Crown copyright 2015 www.justice.gov.uk
Howard League for Penal Reform, www.howardleague.org

Attitudes to sexual violence

Most people do not blame the victim - yet some still do, especially the youngest and oldest age groups

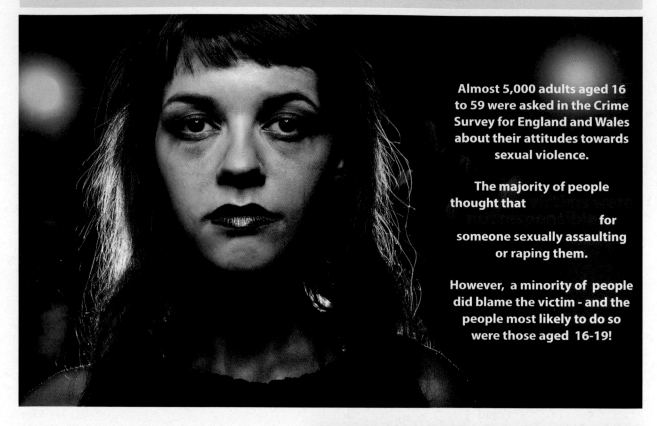

Almost 5,000 adults aged 16 to 59 were asked in the Crime Survey for England and Wales about their attitudes towards sexual violence.

The majority of people thought that victims were not responsible for someone sexually assaulting or raping them.

However, a minority of people did blame the victim - and the people most likely to do so were those aged 16-19!

Rape and other forms of sexual violence are understandably topics that many people find difficult to talk about. But ... myths and misinformation are common.

Myths are also fuelled by ill-informed or unbalanced media reporting of sexual violence-related stories.

Rape Crisis England & Wales and its member Rape Crisis organisations are committed to dispelling myths and raising awareness and understanding of sexual violence, as well as providing services to survivors.

Drinking is not a crime.
Rape is.

No matter how much she's drunk...
No matter what she's wearing...
No matter if you've already kissed...
... sex without consent is rape.

If there's any doubt about whether a woman has drunk too much to give consent, assume she hasn't given it.

Responsibility for rape will always lie with the rapist.

Find your local Rape Crisis Centre at www.rapecrisis.org.uk or call Rape Crisis freephone helpline 0808 802 9999
(12n-2.30pm / 7-9.30pm every day)

**Overall most people agree that the victim is not responsible
for someone sexually assaulting or raping them.**

Percentage saying the victim is / is not responsible

While under the influence of drugs

60.0

23.0

8.0

9.0

| Completely/ mostly responsible | A little bit responsible | Not responsible | Don't know |

But amongst 16-19 year olds only 48% agreed that the victim was not responsible

MYTH: *Someone who has willingly drunk lots of alcohol or taken drugs shouldn't then complain about being raped.*

FACT: *In law, consent must be fully and freely given by someone with the capacity to do so. If a person is unconscious or incapacitated by alcohol or drugs, they are unable to give their consent to sex. Having sex with a person who is incapacitated through alcohol or drugs is therefore rape.*

Percentage saying the victim is / is not responsible

While drunk

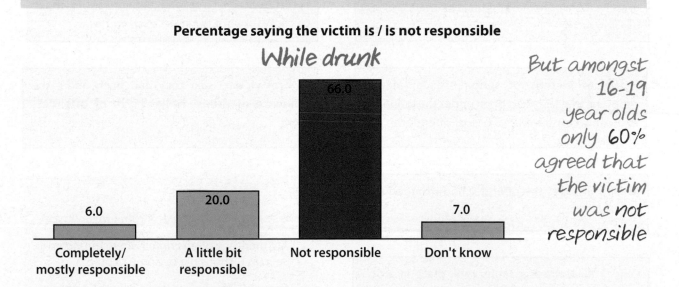

66.0

20.0

6.0

7.0

| Completely/ mostly responsible | A little bit responsible | Not responsible | Don't know |

But amongst 16-19 year olds only 60% agreed that the victim was not responsible

*No one should feel that they are to blame for a rape or sexual assault...
Our main concern is that the crime is reported and that you receive the specialist care you deserve. Nobody will judge you.*

Metropolitan police

If they have been flirting heavily with the person beforehand

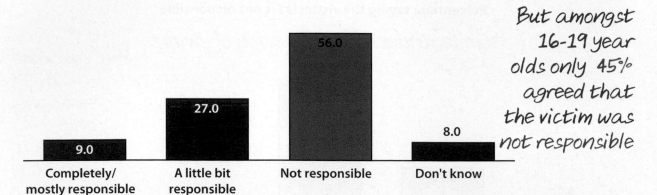

Completely/ mostly responsible	A little bit responsible	Not responsible	Don't know
9.0	27.0	56.0	8.0

But amongst 16-19 year olds only 45% agreed that the victim was not responsible

MYTH: If two people have had sex with each other before, it's always OK to have sex again.

FACT: Even if a person is in a relationship with someone or has had sex with them before, this does not mean that they cannot be sexually assaulted or raped by that person. Consent must be given and received every time two people engage in sexual contact.

Some statistics:

In 2013/14, **3.6%** of men and **19.9%** of women reported that they had been the victim of some form of sexual assault after they reached the age of 16.

Sexual offences recorded by the police have increased. This may reflect improvements in recording and/or a greater willingness of victims to come forward to report such crimes.

29% of victims of serious sexual assault reported that they had been under the influence of alcohol compared to **36%** of offenders.

3% of victims said they had been under the influence of drugs, while **10%** of offenders were.

In **6%** of cases the offender had drugged the victim.

Some issues

- Is sexual assault different from other crimes?

- Are there any other crimes where the victim is seen as responsible by some people?

Only **1%** of these assaults took place in a pub club or disco while **38%** were in the victim's own home. **24%** were at the offender's home.

- Can you offer any reasons why the attitudes of young people are different from the majority?

- Do you think that attitudes to sexual assault and ways of dealing with it have changed over time?

67% of victims told someone about the incident - usually a friend or a relative. Only **17%** told the police.

Source: Crime Statistics, Focus on Violent Crime and Sexual Offences, 2013/14 © Office for National Statistics 2015
www.ons.gov.uk
rapecrisis.org.uk

Victims of fraud

Identity crime is growing in the UK and young people are amongst the targets

Your identity is valuable

Without it, many of the things we take for granted on a day to day basis would be impossible to get ie bank accounts, passports, driving licences, mobile phone contracts etc. All of these depend on being able to prove who you are.

Identity crime remains the biggest fraud threat.

What is Identity Crime?

Identity Fraud: a criminal **makes up an identity** - often involving forged documents - or **pretends to be someone else** - to get products or services.

When a criminal uses a **real person's details** to impersonate them and open new accounts, this is called **identity theft**.

A victim of **identity theft** often finds that money has been removed from their bank, a fraudulent passport or driving licence has been created in their name, or loans, mortgages and mobile phone contracts have been set-up using their identity.

There were **105,500 victims** of all types of **identity fraud** in 2014 and almost **114,000 instances** were recorded.

Facility Takeover Fraud: a fraudster obtains enough details (like passwords) to bypass security on your existing accounts and take them over.

There were **18,873 victims of facility take over fraud** in 2014.

41% of all fraud is identity fraud... and numbers are increasing

The greatest increase was where a fictitious or stolen identity was used to obtain bank accounts. There were **23,686** cases in 2014 compared with **12,544** in 2013 - **up 89%**.

Anyone can be a victim...

The average age of a victim of ID fraud is **46**, with men being **1.7 times** more likely than women to have their identity stolen.

In 2014, there were increases in all victim age groups over 21.

However young people are increasingly becoming targets - the number of young adult **identity fraud** victims aged between 21 and 30 years of age has increased by **51.7%** since 2011 from **9,789** to **14,850**.

A survey showed that **a third** of UK adults were failing to take basic security measures to protect their identities from fraudsters eg

Online security - 34% DO NOT regularly update their firewall or antivirus software

Social media - 35% DO NOT limit the amount of information they share

Safe disposal of documents - 31% DO NOT shred letters before throwing them away

Which of the following security measures, if any, do you REGULARLY take?

(Base: 4,061 GB adults aged 18+)

Measure	%
Locking all doors and windows	85%
Cutting up old credit and debit cards	85%
Shredding letters before throwing them away	69%
Updating computer's firewall, anti-virus and anti-spyware	66%
Limiting the amount of personal information on social networking sites	65%
Not writing down passwords or PINs	61%
Deleting web browser history and cookies	57%
Not posting holiday pictures on social network	37%
Redirecting post for at least six months when moving house	29%
NONE of these	3%

The **Not With My Name** Campaign targets the growing threat of identity crime in the UK

NOT WITH MY NAME

PROTECT YOUR PERSONAL INFORMATION

CITY OF LONDON POLICE
National Policing Lead for Fraud

ActionFraud
National Fraud & Cyber Crime Reporting Centre
actionfraud.police.uk

CRIMESTOPPERS
0800 555 111

Age differences

95% of those aged 65+ said they cut up old credit and debit cards, compared to just **66%** of 18-24 year-olds.

Similarly, **83%** of those aged 65+ said they shredded letters, compared to just **45%** of 18-24 year-olds.

Be aware what you share

Your social media profiles can make you a target - just a single piece of personal information, such as your date of birth, can be used to commit fraud in your name.

The Rise of the Vishing Scam

Fraudsters are finding it increasingly difficult to gain access to existing accounts so they are using other methods.

They are now convincing their victims to just give them the money directly. This kind of fraud is called **vishing**.

This is how it works

The fraudster rings you, saying they are from their bank or the police and that your account is at risk - from fraud!

To convince you they are genuine, the caller will suggest you hang up and call the bank back on the number printed on the back of your debit or credit card.

You get through to someone who seems to be from the bank and helpfully says they will set up a safe account for you to transfer your money into.

But even though you called the real number you are still speaking to someone from the fraudster's team because the fraudster never actually disconnects the line.

If you trust what the fraudster has told you and transfer the money, in most cases you will never see it again.

Getting your money back

If a fraudster gains access to a bank account and transfers the balance to another account, then the bank must pay the money back to their customer.

But in cases of **vishing**, the customer has **voluntarily** transferred their own money to the fraudster. The bank has done nothing wrong and is under no legal obligation to repay the customer.

A bank would NEVER ask you to transfer funds into a 'safe account' even if there was a breach

2,029 GB adults aged 18+ who were bank account holders were asked:
"Would you authorise a transfer of your money into another safe account allocated by your bank to protect your funds while they investigated a breach?"

Age groups saying they WOULD authorise a transfer

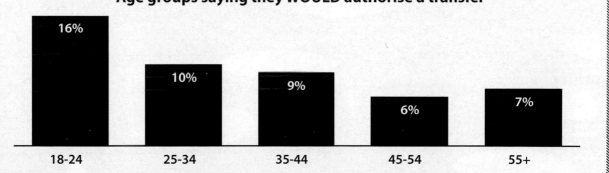

18-24	25-34	35-44	45-54	55+
16%	10%	9%	6%	7%

If you suspect you have become the victim of fraud contact your bank and Action Fraud:
Tel: 0300 123 2040
www.actionfraud.police.uk

Other useful information:
www.getsafeonline.org
Know Fraud, No Fraud campaign
www.knowfraud.co.uk
Not with my name
www.actionfraud.police.uk/resources-and-campaigns/not-with-my-name

Some issues

- Why are younger people less careful about fraud?

- How much information have you given away on your social media accounts?

- What should be done to make sure people are more aware of fraud prevention?

Source: Cifas www.cifas.org.uk
Comres survey on Identity Fraud
on behalf of Cifas www.comres.co.uk
BBA www.bba.org.uk
YouGov www.yougov.co.uk

Religion

Religion in Britain

The Church of England's decline has continued over the last decade

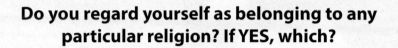

A survey of 2,878 adults in Britain showed that the proportion who say they are Anglican has fallen **40%** in the last ten years, down from **13 million** people to about **8.5 million**.

Do you regard yourself as belonging to any particular religion? If YES, which?

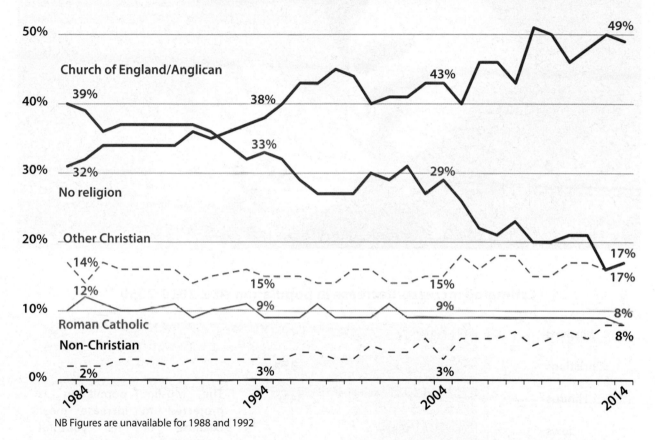

NB Figures are unavailable for 1988 and 1992

In the past, religion played a more prominent role in people's identity than it does today.

The main reason for the increase in British people saying they are NOT religious is that each generation is less religious than the next - as older generations die, the overall population becomes less religious. This is known as generational displacement.

While the percentage of Anglicans is declining, other religions are maintaining or increasing their percentages.

Some issues

- How much does religion matter in Britain?

- The Church of England plays a part in the government of the country because 26 bishops have seats in the House of Lords. Is this still justified?

- 49% of people say they are not religious. How much will Britain change if, as seems likely, that becomes a majority?

- In your experience, is each generation less religious than the last one?

Source: British Social Attitudes Survey, NatCen 2015 www.natcen.ac.uk

World religions

The religious profile of the world is changing

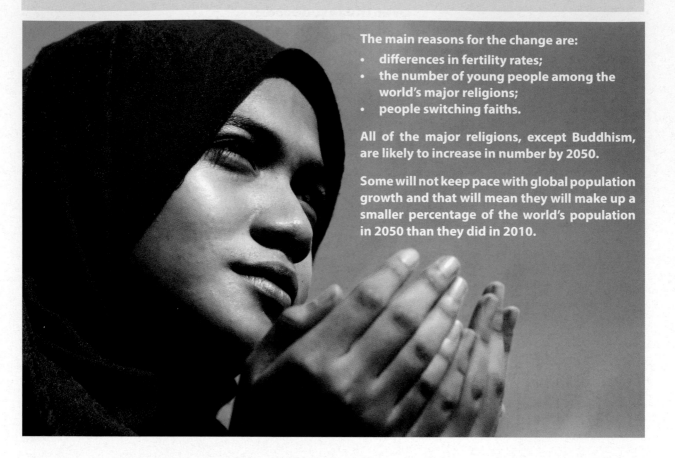

The main reasons for the change are:

- differences in fertility rates;
- the number of young people among the world's major religions;
- people switching faiths.

All of the major religions, except Buddhism, are likely to increase in number by 2050.

Some will not keep pace with global population growth and that will mean they will make up a smaller percentage of the world's population in 2050 than they did in 2010.

Estimated increase/decrease in population size, 2010-2050

Muslims	73%
Christians	35%
Hindus	34%
Jews	16%
Folk religions*	11%
Unaffiliated*	9%
Other religions*	6%
Buddhists	-0.3%

35% growth in overall global population

The Muslim population is projected to increase most because of its youthful population and high fertility rates.

The number of Christians is projected to rise at about the same rate as the global population.

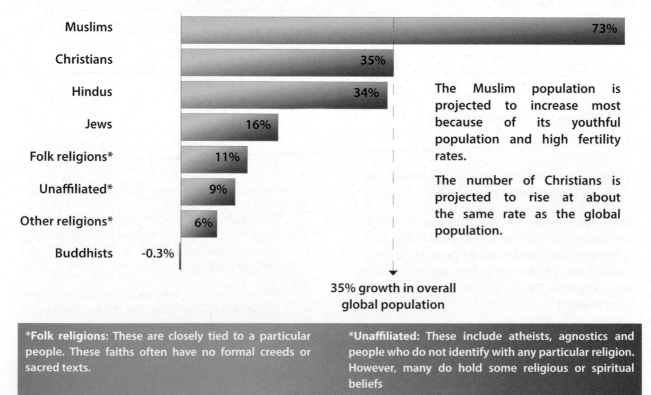

*Folk religions: These are closely tied to a particular people. These faiths often have no formal creeds or sacred texts.

*Unaffiliated: These include atheists, agnostics and people who do not identify with any particular religion. However, many do hold some religious or spiritual beliefs

*Other religions: Groups not classified elsewhere.

Projected change in global population - Christians & Muslims

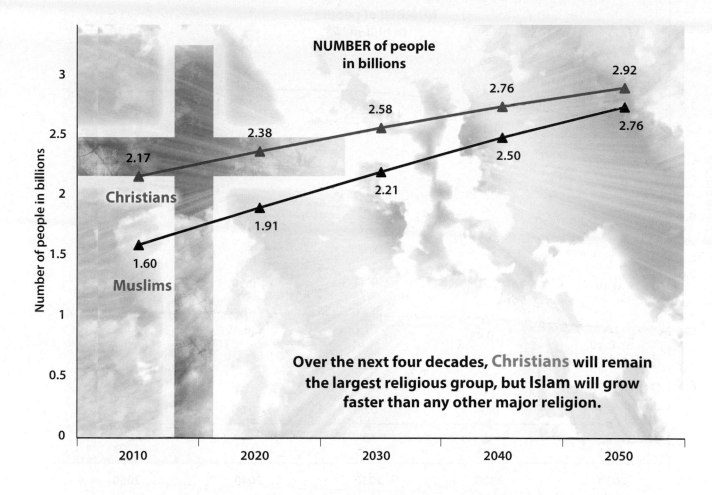

NUMBER of people in billions

Number of people in billions

- 3
- 2.5
- 2
- 1.5
- 1
- 0.5
- 0

Christians: 2.17 (2010), 2.38 (2020), 2.58 (2030), 2.76 (2040), 2.92 (2050)

Muslims: 1.60 (2010), 1.91 (2020), 2.21 (2030), 2.50 (2040), 2.76 (2050)

2010 · 2020 · 2030 · 2040 · 2050

Over the next four decades, Christians will remain the largest religious group, but Islam will grow faster than any other major religion.

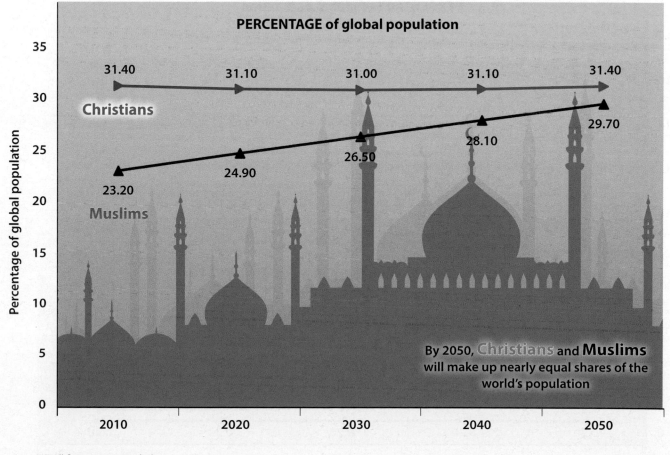

PERCENTAGE of global population

Percentage of global population

- 35
- 30
- 25
- 20
- 15
- 10
- 5
- 0

Christians: 31.40 (2010), 31.10 (2020), 31.00 (2030), 31.10 (2040), 31.40 (2050)

Muslims: 23.20 (2010), 24.90 (2020), 26.50 (2030), 28.10 (2040), 29.70 (2050)

2010 · 2020 · 2030 · 2040 · 2050

By 2050, Christians and Muslims will make up nearly equal shares of the world's population

NB All figures are rounded

Projected change in global population, all other religions

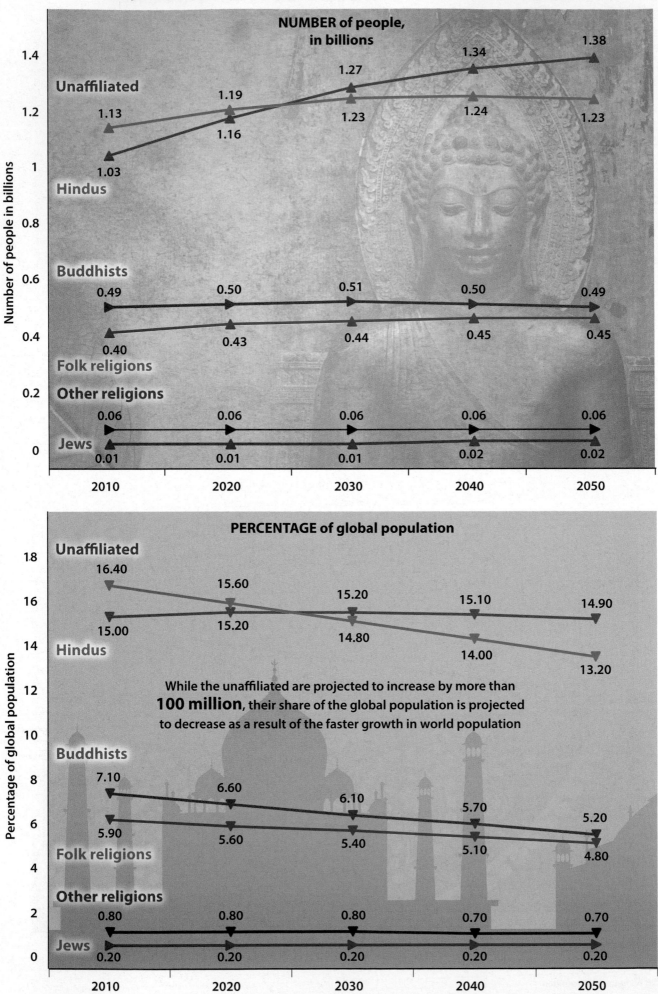

NUMBER of people, in billions

Number of people in billions

Unaffiliated
- 1.13
- 1.19
- 1.27
- 1.34
- 1.38

Hindus
- 1.03
- 1.16
- 1.23
- 1.24
- 1.23

Buddhists
- 0.49
- 0.50
- 0.51
- 0.50
- 0.49

Folk religions
- 0.40
- 0.43
- 0.44
- 0.45
- 0.45

Other religions
- 0.06
- 0.06
- 0.06
- 0.06
- 0.06

Jews
- 0.01
- 0.01
- 0.01
- 0.02
- 0.02

2010 2020 2030 2040 2050

PERCENTAGE of global population

Percentage of global population

Unaffiliated
- 16.40
- 15.60
- 15.20
- 15.10
- 14.90

Hindus
- 15.00
- 15.20
- 14.80
- 14.00
- 13.20

While the unaffiliated are projected to increase by more than **100 million**, their share of the global population is projected to decrease as a result of the faster growth in world population

Buddhists
- 7.10
- 6.60
- 6.10
- 5.70
- 5.20

Folk religions
- 5.90
- 5.60
- 5.40
- 5.10
- 4.80

Other religions
- 0.80
- 0.80
- 0.80
- 0.70
- 0.70

Jews
- 0.20
- 0.20
- 0.20
- 0.20
- 0.20

2010 2020 2030 2040 2050

Switching faiths

In some countries, it is fairly common for adults to leave their childhood religion and switch to another faith.

Christians are expected to experience the largest net losses from switching.

106 million are projected to leave, with most joining the ranks of the religiously unaffiliated.

Globally, about **40 million** people are projected to switch into Christianity.

Changing religious majorities

Several countries are projected to have a different religious majority in 2050 than they did in 2010. The number of countries with Christian majorities is expected to decline from 159 to 151, as Christians are projected to drop below 50% of the population in these countries.

Countries That Will No Longer Have a Christian Majority in 2050

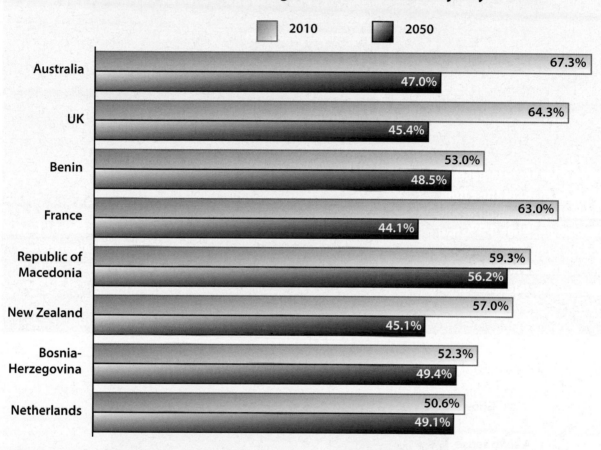

Country	2010	2050
Australia	67.3%	47.0%
UK	64.3%	45.4%
Benin	53.0%	48.5%
France	63.0%	44.1%
Republic of Macedonia	59.3%	56.2%
New Zealand	57.0%	45.1%
Bosnia-Herzegovina	52.3%	49.4%
Netherlands	50.6%	49.1%

If current trends continue, by 2050...

- Muslims are expected to make up **more than 50%** of the population in 51 countries as both the Republic of Macedonia and Nigeria are projected to gain Muslim majorities.

- Nigeria also will continue to have a very large Christian population - it will have the third-largest Christian population in the world by 2050, after the United States and Brazil.

- India will retain a Hindu majority but also will have the largest Muslim population of any country in the world, surpassing Indonesia.

- **40%** of Christians in the world will live in sub-Saharan Africa.

Some issues

- Why do you think people 'drift' away from some but not from other religions?

- Does it matter what the majority religion is in a country?

- Does it matter what the majority religion is in the world?

- How much does religion affect your everyday life?

Source: The Future of World Religions: Population Growth Projections 2010-2050, Pew Research Center www.pewresearch.org

Beliefs

Superstition and the supernatural... what do people believe?

A survey of 2,000 UK adults aged 18 and over revealed that **55%** believed in supernatural phenomena and superstitions compared to **49%** who believed in a God.

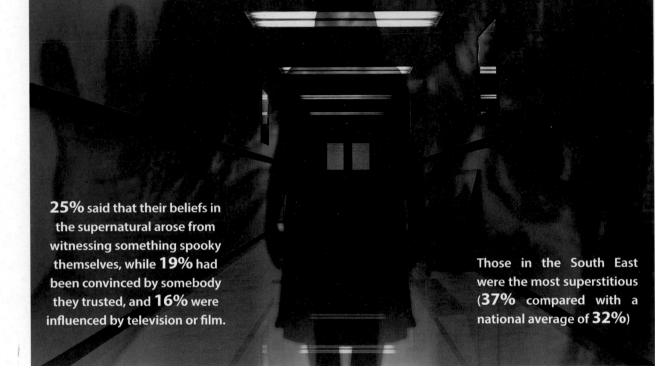

25% said that their beliefs in the supernatural arose from witnessing something spooky themselves, while **19%** had been convinced by somebody they trusted, and **16%** were influenced by television or film.

Those in the South East were the most superstitious (**37%** compared with a national average of **32%**)

Top 10 beliefs in unexplained phenomena

Belief	%
Ghosts	33%
A sixth sense	32%
UFOs	22%
Past lives	19%
Telepathy	18%
Ability to predict the future	18%
Psychic healing	16%
Astrology	10%
Bermuda Triangle	9%
Demons	8%

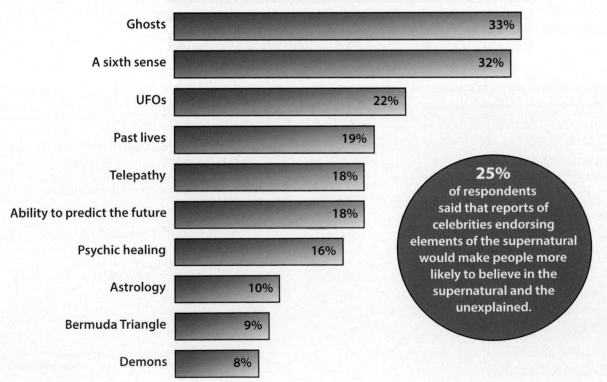

25% of respondents said that reports of celebrities endorsing elements of the supernatural would make people more likely to believe in the supernatural and the unexplained.

Spending on supernatural

4% of people admitted to spending **more than £100** a year.

The Northern Irish were more likely to spend **in excess of £150** hiring the services of someone who claimed to have supernatural powers **7%**.

Supernatural powers

10% claimed to possess at least one supernatural power themselves (mostly seeing into the future, regressing to past lives, or telepathy).

Those in the North West were the most likely to believe that they had a special 'gift' - **14%**.

This was more than attended religious services on a weekly basis - **8%**.

The 10 most common superstitions

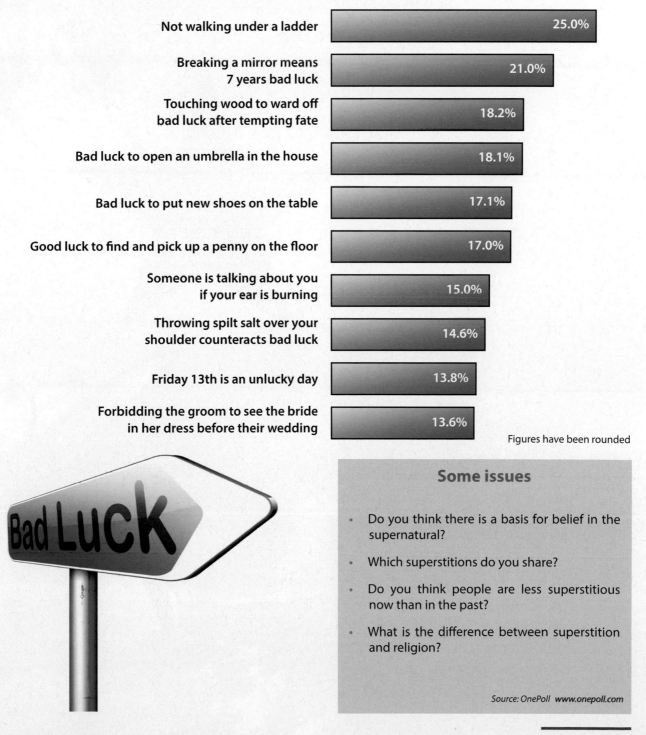

Superstition	%
Not walking under a ladder	25.0%
Breaking a mirror means 7 years bad luck	21.0%
Touching wood to ward off bad luck after tempting fate	18.2%
Bad luck to open an umbrella in the house	18.1%
Bad luck to put new shoes on the table	17.1%
Good luck to find and pick up a penny on the floor	17.0%
Someone is talking about you if your ear is burning	15.0%
Throwing spilt salt over your shoulder counteracts bad luck	14.6%
Friday 13th is an unlucky day	13.8%
Forbidding the groom to see the bride in her dress before their wedding	13.6%

Figures have been rounded

Some issues

- Do you think there is a basis for belief in the supernatural?

- Which superstitions do you share?

- Do you think people are less superstitious now than in the past?

- What is the difference between superstition and religion?

Source: OnePoll www.onepoll.com

War &
conflict

Forced to flee

The number of people being displaced as a result of persecution, conflict, violence or human rights abuses is the highest on record

In 2014, **13.9 million people** were **newly displaced**.

42,500 people per day were forced to leave their homes and seek protection elsewhere, either **within the borders of their countries** or **in other countries**.

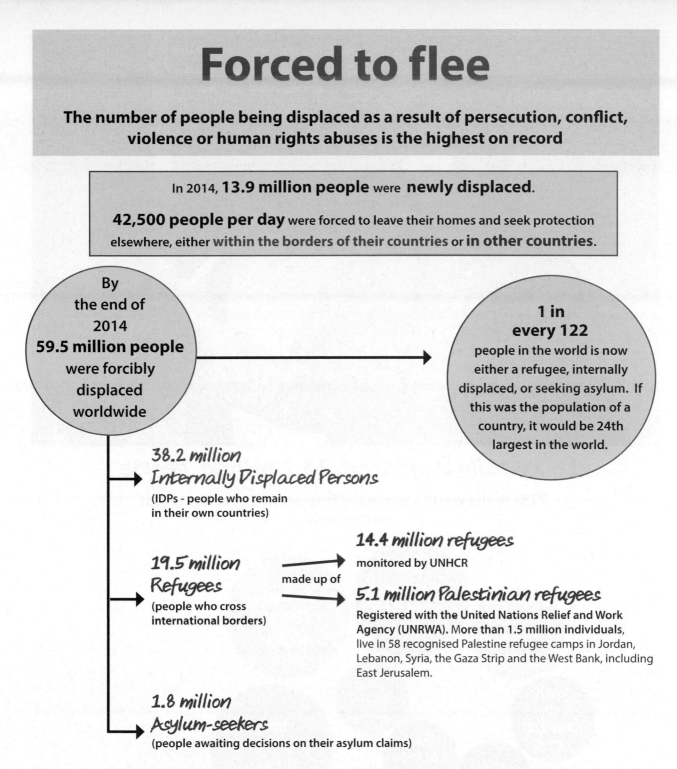

By the end of 2014 **59.5 million people** were forcibly displaced worldwide

1 in every 122 people in the world is now either a refugee, internally displaced, or seeking asylum. If this was the population of a country, it would be 24th largest in the world.

38.2 million Internally Displaced Persons
(IDPs - people who remain in their own countries)

19.5 million Refugees
(people who cross international borders)

made up of

14.4 million refugees
monitored by UNHCR

5.1 million Palestinian refugees
Registered with the United Nations Relief and Work Agency (UNRWA). More than 1.5 million individuals, live in 58 recognised Palestine refugee camps in Jordan, Lebanon, Syria, the Gaza Strip and the West Bank, including East Jerusalem.

1.8 million Asylum-seekers
(people awaiting decisions on their asylum claims)

Conflict leads to more displaced people:

In the past five years, at least 15 conflicts have broken out or re-started:

8 in **Africa** (Côte d'Ivoire, Central African Republic, Libya, Mali, North Eastern Nigeria, Democratic Republic of Congo, South Sudan and, in 2015, Burundi)

3 in the **Middle East** (Syria, Iraq and Yemen)

1 in **Europe** (Ukraine); and

3 in **Asia** (Kyrgyzstan and in several areas of Myanmar and Pakistan)

Long term instability and conflict in Afghanistan, Somalia and elsewhere means that millions of people remain on the move or stranded for years as internally displaced or refugees.

In nearly **90%** of the 60 countries and territories monitored by the UNHCR (UN High Commissioner for Refugees) there were people who had been displaced for ten years or more.

Mali: This little boy is one of the **230,000** internally displaced persons in the country.

UNHCR/H. Caux

Internally Displaced: 38.2 million people

77% of the world's Internally Displaced People live in just ten countries

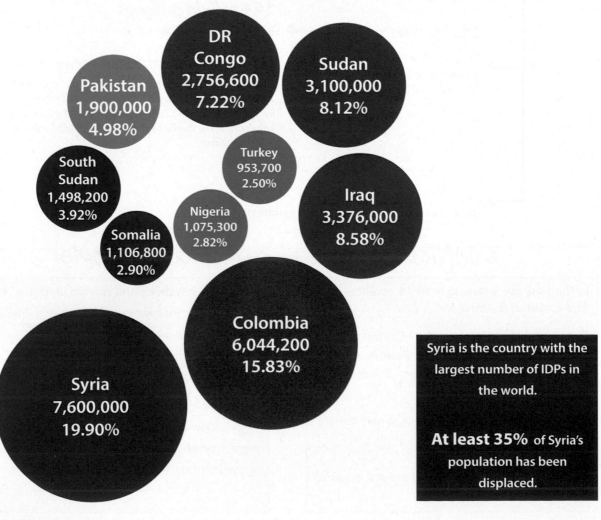

DR Congo
2,756,600
7.22%

Sudan
3,100,000
8.12%

Pakistan
1,900,000
4.98%

South Sudan
1,498,200
3.92%

Turkey
953,700
2.50%

Iraq
3,376,000
8.58%

Nigeria
1,075,300
2.82%

Somalia
1,106,800
2.90%

Colombia
6,044,200
15.83%

Syria
7,600,000
19.90%

Syria is the country with the largest number of IDPs in the world.

At least 35% of Syria's population has been displaced.

Newly displaced

The number of people **newly displaced** during 2014 was the highest in ten years - **11 million.**

30,000 people fleeing per day.

60% of new displacements took place in just five countries:

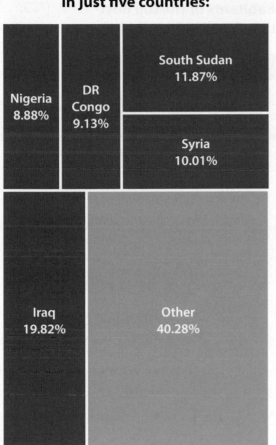

Nigeria 8.88%

DR Congo 9.13%

South Sudan 11.87%

Syria 10.01%

Iraq 19.82%

Other 40.28%

Iraq suffered most **new displacement** with at least **2.2 million** people fleeing from areas that fell under Islamic State (ISIL) control.

Displacement took place for the first time in Ukraine, and data became available for El Salvador for the first time - these two countries accounted for at least **935,400 new displacements** between them. The figure for Ukraine alone was **at least 646,500.**

"The longer a conflict lasts, the more insecure [internally displaced people] feel and when hopelessness sets in, many will cross borders and become refugees"

Volker Türk, Assistant High Commissioner for Protection, UNHCR

A young Syrian refugee carries his brother across the border between Greece and Macedonia, near Eidomeni, Greece
© UNHCR/Andrew McConnell

Refugees: 14.4 million

(monitored by the UNHCR)

Lebanon hosted the largest number of refugees compared to its national population - in other words **almost one in four** inhabitants of Lebanon was a refugee at the end of 2014.

Number of refugees per 1,000 inhabitants of the top host countries compared to their national population, 2014

Lebanon	232
Jordan	87
Nauru	39
Chad	34
Djibouti	23
South Sudan	21
Turkey	21
Mauritania	19
Sweden	15
Malta	14

Developing regions hosted **12.4 million people -** **86%** of the world's refugees.

For the first time, **Turkey** became the largest refugee-hosting country worldwide, with **1.59 million** refugees.

Age groups of refugees

51% of refugees were **under 18 years old** - the highest figure in more than a decade.

46% were aged **18-59** and **3%** were **over 60**.

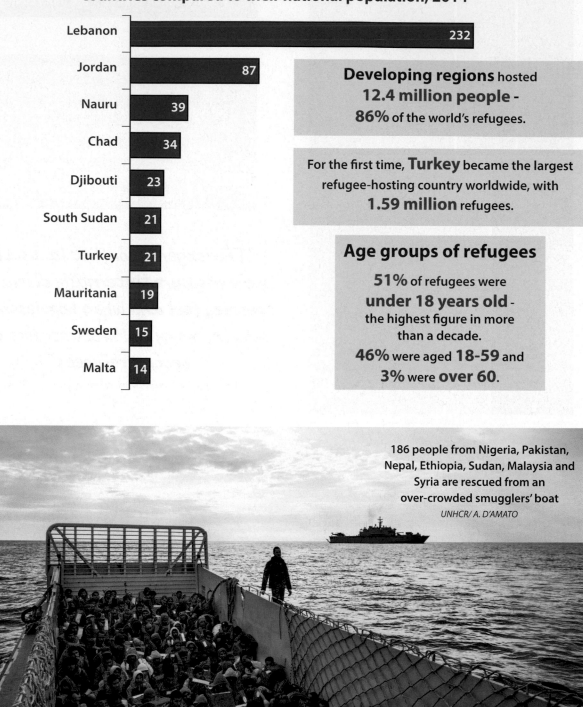

186 people from Nigeria, Pakistan, Nepal, Ethiopia, Sudan, Malaysia and Syria are rescued from an over-crowded smugglers' boat

UNHCR/ A. D'AMATO

As a result of conflicts and suffering around the world, there has been a dramatic growth in the number of refugees seeking safety by taking dangerous sea journeys.

In Europe, **more than 219,000** refugees and migrants crossed the Mediterranean Sea during 2014 - three times more than the previous high point in 2011.

Syrian refugee, Ahmed, 7, rests at a train station in Macedonia.

© UNHCR/Andrew McConnell

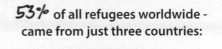

Where the refugees came from

53% of all refugees worldwide - came from just three countries:

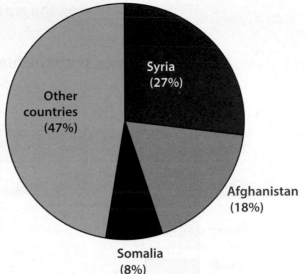

- Syria (27%)
- Afghanistan (18%)
- Somalia (8%)
- Other countries (47%)

With **3.88 million refugees** in **107 countries**, Syria became the world's top source country of refugees.

Just three years ago Syria did not feature even in the top 30 source countries for refugees. This shows how rapidly the situation in that country has deteriorated.

Adding the estimated **7.6 million** persons displaced within the country makes Syrians the largest displaced population worldwide.

Today, on average, almost **one out of every four** refugees is Syrian, with **95%** located in surrounding countries.

NB all figures are rounded

Where the refugees returned to

Only 126,800 refugees from **37 countries** were reported to have returned home in 2014 - this was the lowest level of refugee returns since 1983.

The countries that reported the largest numbers included:

The Democratic Republic of the Congo	**25,200**
Mali	**21,000**
Afghanistan	**17,800**
Angola	**14,300**
Sudan	**13,100**
Côte d'Ivoire	**12,400**
Iraq	**10,900**
Rwanda	**5,800**

These eight countries combined accounted for **95%** of total refugee returns during the year.

Some issues

- What should be done to help refugees?

- Can individuals like us do more to help refugees around the world?

- Why is shelter for refugees mainly being provided by developing countries?

- What long-term measures could other countries provide to ease the situation and avoid further displacement of people?

Source: Internal Displacement Monitoring Centre (IDCM)
Global overview 2015 www.internal-displacement.org
UNHCR www.unhcr.org.uk

Military spending

How much money the world spends on all military purposes

15 countries with the highest military expenditure in 2014
$US billions

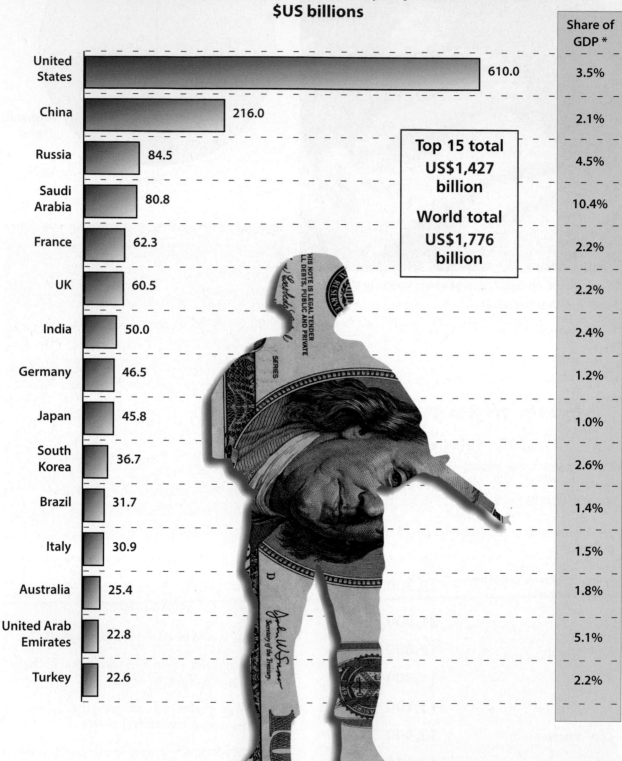

Country	$US billions	Share of GDP *
United States	610.0	3.5%
China	216.0	2.1%
Russia	84.5	4.5%
Saudi Arabia	80.8	10.4%
France	62.3	2.2%
UK	60.5	2.2%
India	50.0	2.4%
Germany	46.5	1.2%
Japan	45.8	1.0%
South Korea	36.7	2.6%
Brazil	31.7	1.4%
Italy	30.9	1.5%
Australia	25.4	1.8%
United Arab Emirates	22.8	5.1%
Turkey	22.6	2.2%

Top 15 total US$1,427 billion

World total US$1,776 billion

*GDP - Gross Domestic Product is the market value of all officially recognised final goods and services produced within a country in a given period of time. GDP per head is a useful indicator of a country's standard of living

NB Figures for China, Russia, Germany and United Arab Emirates (UAE) are estimates

Military burden

A country's military expenditure as a share of GDP is known as the **military burden**.

In 2014 about **55%** of countries with data had military burdens **below 1.5%** of GDP.

However, in 2014 there was a sharp increase in the number of countries with a burden of **over 4%** of GDP, as well as in countries with military burdens **over 5%**.

20 countries had a military burden of **4%** in 2014 (or in the most recent year data was available). These countries were concentrated in Africa, Eastern Europe and the Middle East. The majority were involved in armed conflict or had a recent history of armed conflict.

10 had military burdens over **5%** - Algeria, Libya, Angola, Chad, Congo, South Sudan, Israel, Oman, Saudi Arabia and UAE.

The share of world military expenditure of the 15 states with the highest expenditure in 2014 compared to the rest of the world

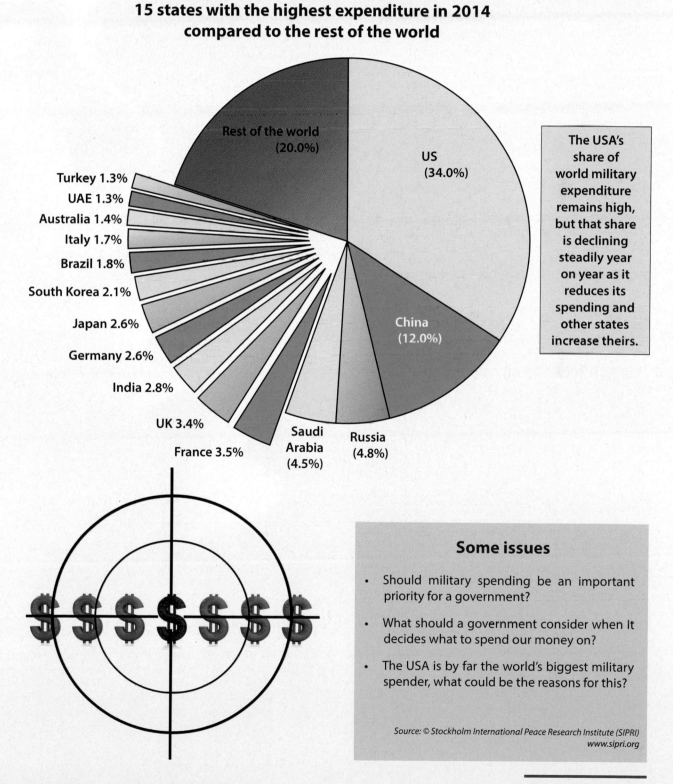

Rest of the world (20.0%)

US (34.0%)

Turkey 1.3%
UAE 1.3%
Australia 1.4%
Italy 1.7%
Brazil 1.8%
South Korea 2.1%
Japan 2.6%
Germany 2.6%
India 2.8%
UK 3.4%
France 3.5%
Saudi Arabia (4.5%)
Russia (4.8%)
China (12.0%)

The USA's share of world military expenditure remains high, but that share is declining steadily year on year as it reduces its spending and other states increase theirs.

Some issues

- Should military spending be an important priority for a government?

- What should a government consider when it decides what to spend our money on?

- The USA is by far the world's biggest military spender, what could be the reasons for this?

Source: © Stockholm International Peace Research Institute (SIPRI) www.sipri.org

Wider world

The world as 100 people

A simple way to picture our complex world

The 100 People Foundation helps us to understand the issues facing our planet and the resources we share by imagining the world more simply as if it was 100 people.

When the world population reached the milestone of 7 billion people they updated their original 2006 statistics.

IF THE WORLD WAS 100 PEOPLE THERE WOULD BE...

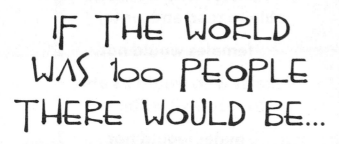

50 Females & 50 Males

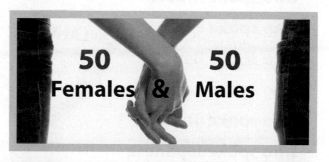

26 children aged 0-14 and

66 adults aged 15-64

8 adults would be 65+

33 Christians **22** Muslims

14 Hindus **7** Buddhists

12 people who practise other religions

12 people who would not be aligned with a religion

60 Asians **15** Africans

11 people from Europe

9 from Latin America & the Caribbean

5 people from North America

51 urban dwellers **49** rural dwellers

THERE WOULD BE...

12 who spoke Chinese

5 who spoke Spanish

5 who spoke English

3 who spoke Arabic

3 who spoke Hindi

3 who spoke Bengali

3 who spoke Portuguese

2 who spoke Russian

2 who spoke Japanese

62 who spoke other languages

83 who would be able to read and write;

17 who would not

79 females who would be able to read and write;

21 females would not

88 males who would be able to read and write;

12 males would not

---

75 would be mobile phone users

25 would not

30 would be internet users

70 would not

22 would own or share a computer

78 would not

---

76 eligible males would have a primary school education

72 eligible females would have a primary school education

66 eligible males would have a secondary school education

63 eligible females would have a secondary school education

7 people would have a degree

1 would be dying of starvation

15 would be undernourished

21 would be overweight

63 would have adequate nutrition

All photos posed by models

77
would have a place to shelter from the wind and rain

23
would not

87
would have access to safe drinking water

13
would have no clean, safe water to drink

48
would live on less than $2 USD per day

1 out of 2
children would live in poverty

78
would have electricity

22
would not

Some issues

- Do these figures match up to how you imagine the world?

- How does this compare to the country you live in?

- And the continent?

- What is the most surprising number here?

- How does this change the way you see the world?

Source: 100 People Foundation
www.100people.org

Public perceptions

In Great Britain we over-estimate the scale of some issues... but so do other countries

Adults in 14 countries were questioned about the basic make-up of their populations and the scale of key social issues. Respondents in Italy gave the least accurate answers, followed by the US, South Korea, Poland, Hungary, France, Canada, Belgium, Australia, Great Britain, Spain, Japan, and Germany. Sweden gave the most accurate answers

Out of every 100 people...
...how many do you think are Christian?

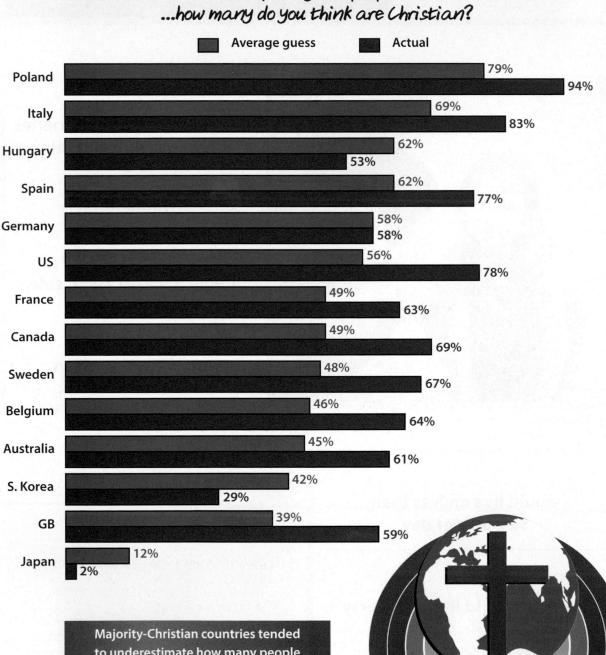

Average guess   Actual

Country	Average guess	Actual
Poland	79%	94%
Italy	69%	83%
Hungary	62%	53%
Spain	62%	77%
Germany	58%	58%
US	56%	78%
France	49%	63%
Canada	49%	69%
Sweden	48%	67%
Belgium	46%	64%
Australia	45%	61%
S. Korea	42%	29%
GB	39%	59%
Japan	12%	2%

Majority-Christian countries tended to underestimate how many people count themselves as Christian. In the 12 majority-Christian countries in the survey, the average guess was **51%**, when the actual proportion counting themselves as Christians was **61%**.

...how many do you think are Muslim?

What percentage of the population do you think are immigrants to this country?

■ Average guess   ■ Actual

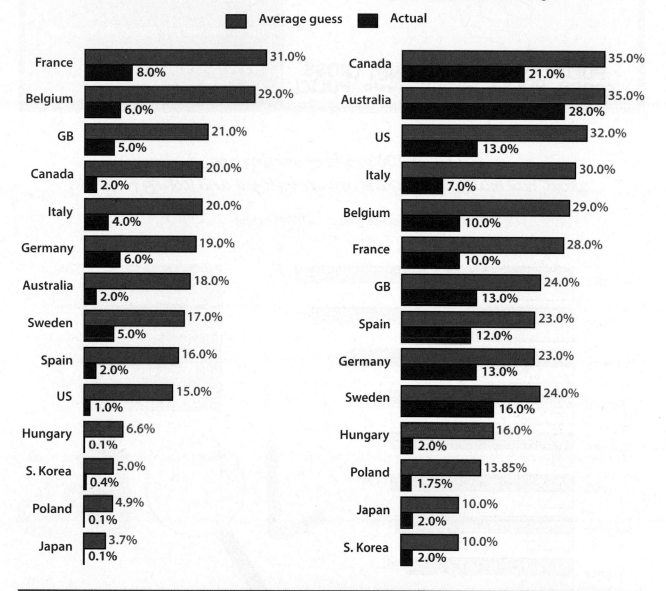

Country	...how many are Muslim?		Country	What % are immigrants?	
	Average guess	Actual		Average guess	Actual
France	31.0%	8.0%	Canada	35.0%	21.0%
Belgium	29.0%	6.0%	Australia	35.0%	28.0%
GB	21.0%	5.0%	US	32.0%	13.0%
Canada	20.0%	2.0%	Italy	30.0%	7.0%
Italy	20.0%	4.0%	Belgium	29.0%	10.0%
Germany	19.0%	6.0%	France	28.0%	10.0%
Australia	18.0%	2.0%	GB	24.0%	13.0%
Sweden	17.0%	5.0%	Spain	23.0%	12.0%
Spain	16.0%	2.0%	Germany	23.0%	13.0%
US	15.0%	1.0%	Sweden	24.0%	16.0%
Hungary	6.6%	0.1%	Hungary	16.0%	2.0%
S. Korea	5.0%	0.4%	Poland	13.85%	1.75%
Poland	4.9%	0.1%	Japan	10.0%	2.0%
Japan	3.7%	0.1%	S. Korea	10.0%	2.0%

Out of 100 eligible voters...
...how many do you think voted in the last election?

Do you think this statement is true or false?
The murder rate is rising

49% of people across the countries thought that the murder rate was rising and only **27%** thought it was falling - when in fact in all countries in the survey, the murder rate was actually falling.

The British were the most likely to have an accurate view of murder rate trends: **49%** thought it was falling and only **25%** thought it was rising.

Out of 100 people of working age...
about how many do you think are unemployed and looking for work?

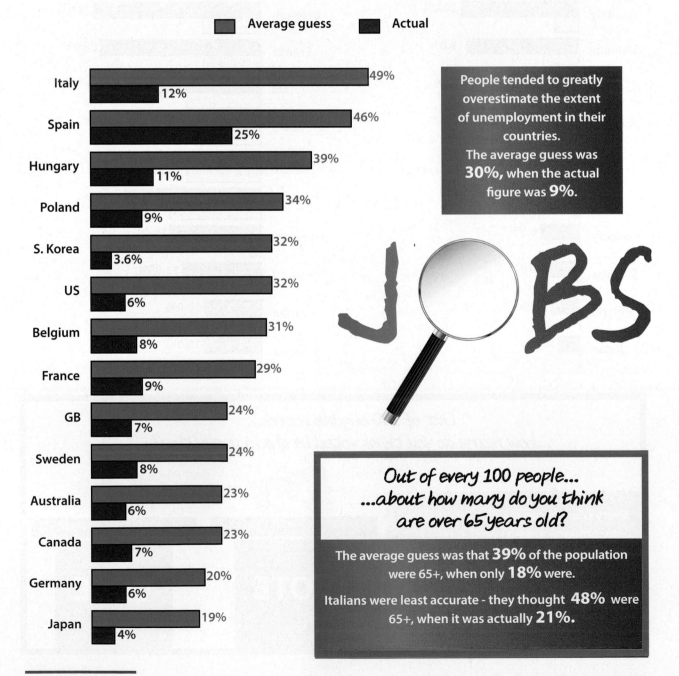

Average guess | Actual

Country	Average guess	Actual
Italy	49%	12%
Spain	46%	25%
Hungary	39%	11%
Poland	34%	9%
S. Korea	32%	3.6%
US	32%	6%
Belgium	31%	8%
France	29%	9%
GB	24%	7%
Sweden	24%	8%
Australia	23%	6%
Canada	23%	7%
Germany	20%	6%
Japan	19%	4%

People tended to greatly overestimate the extent of unemployment in their countries.
The average guess was **30%**, when the actual figure was **9%**.

Out of every 100 people...
...about how many do you think are over 65 years old?

The average guess was that **39%** of the population were 65+, when only **18%** were.

Italians were least accurate - they thought **48%** were 65+, when it was actually **21%**.

In your opinion, what percentage of girls aged between 15 and 19 give birth each year?

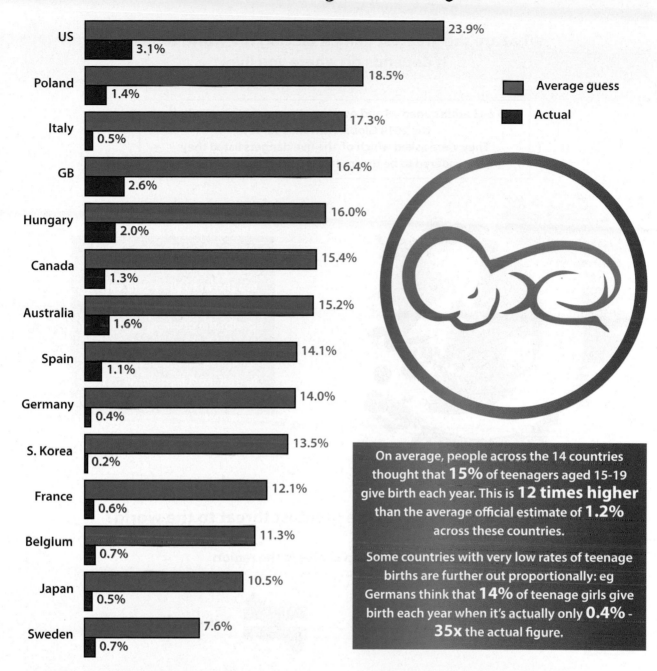

Average guess / **Actual**

Country	Average guess	Actual
US	23.9%	3.1%
Poland	18.5%	1.4%
Italy	17.3%	0.5%
GB	16.4%	2.6%
Hungary	16.0%	2.0%
Canada	15.4%	1.3%
Australia	15.2%	1.6%
Spain	14.1%	1.1%
Germany	14.0%	0.4%
S. Korea	13.5%	0.2%
France	12.1%	0.6%
Belgium	11.3%	0.7%
Japan	10.5%	0.5%
Sweden	7.6%	0.7%

On average, people across the 14 countries thought that **15%** of teenagers aged 15-19 give birth each year. This is **12 times higher** than the average official estimate of **1.2%** across these countries.

Some countries with very low rates of teenage births are further out proportionally: eg Germans think that **14%** of teenage girls give birth each year when it's actually only **0.4%** - **35x** the actual figure.

What do you think the average life expectancy will be of a child born in 2014?

Across the 14 countries, the actual life expectancy was **81 years** - respondents guessed it to be **80 years**.

People in S. Korea guessed it to be **89 years**, compared with an actual of **80 years** for the country.

Hungarians guessed it to be **68 years**, when the average for Hungary was predicted to be **75 years**.

Some issues

- What causes people to have such a false idea about actual figures?

- How can people find actual statistics on these issues?

- Should schools teach people to interpret statistics more accurately?

- Why is knowing the facts about numbers important in each of the areas mentioned?

Base: 11,527 adults were surveyed in 14 countries.

Source: Ipsos MORI Perils of Perception Survey
www.ipsos-mori.com/researchpublications/researcharchive/3466/
Perceptions-are-not-reality-10-things-the-world-gets-wrong.aspx

Global threats

What are the greatest dangers facing the world today?
It depends on where you live!

48,643 adults aged 18 and over, in 44 countries, responded to the 2014 Global Attitudes survey.
They were asked which of the five dangers listed they considered to be the "greatest threat to the world."

Across the nations surveyed, opinions on which was the top threat to the world varied greatly by region and country, eg with the growing conflicts in the Middle East, people in that region named religious & ethnic hatred most frequently as the greatest threat to the world.

Which of these poses the greatest threat to the world?

■ Top choice in the region

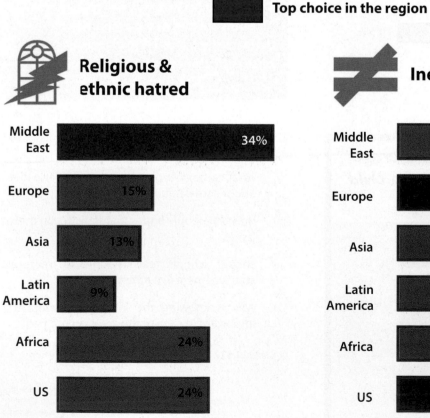

Religious & ethnic hatred

Region	%
Middle East	34%
Europe	15%
Asia	13%
Latin America	9%
Africa	24%
US	24%

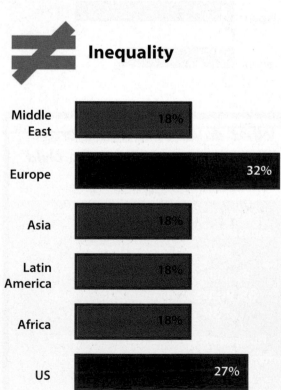

Inequality

Region	%
Middle East	18%
Europe	32%
Asia	18%
Latin America	18%
Africa	18%
US	27%

Top choice in the region

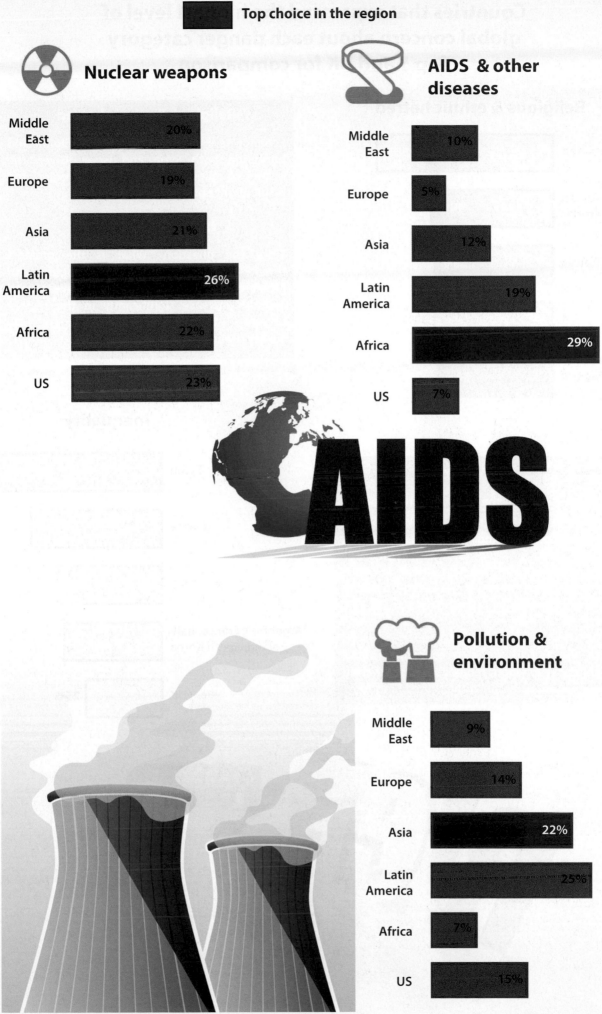

Nuclear weapons

Middle East	20%
Europe	19%
Asia	21%
Latin America	26%
Africa	22%
US	23%

AIDS & other diseases

Middle East	10%
Europe	5%
Asia	12%
Latin America	19%
Africa	29%
US	7%

Pollution & environment

Middle East	9%
Europe	14%
Asia	22%
Latin America	25%
Africa	7%
US	15%

Countries that expressed the highest level of global concern about each danger category
Top 5 and UK for comparison

Religious & ethnic hatred

- Lebanon — 58%
- Palestinian Territories — 40%
- Tunisia — 39%
- UK — 39%
- Nigeria — 38%

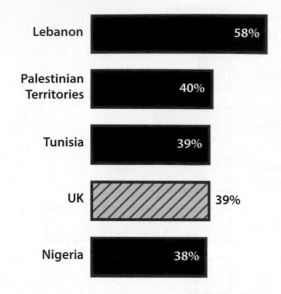

Religious & ethnic hatred

Lebanon is a country divided by religion and bordering both Syria and Israel. Given the history of religious violence in the region, the result might not be surprising.

Increase in concern

Since the question "What is the greatest threat?" was last asked in 2007, religious and ethnic conflicts in Syria and Iraq have caused fears to increase significantly in the region: Lebanon +19 percentage points, Egypt +18, Turkey +9 and Jordan +6.

Inequality

The gap between the rich and the poor is increasingly considered as the world's top problem by people living in developed countries.

Since the question was last asked in 2007, inequality has been a growing concern: Spain +27 percentage points, Italy +16, UK +11, France +8, Germany +7.

While the British are also concerned about inequality, fears about religious & ethnic hatred are even more common in the United Kingdom.

Inequality

- Spain — 54%
- Greece — 43%
- Germany — 34%
- Argentina, France, Italy Poland, South Korea — 32%
- UK — 25%

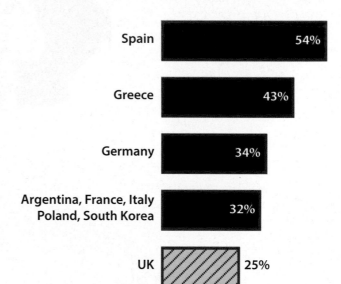

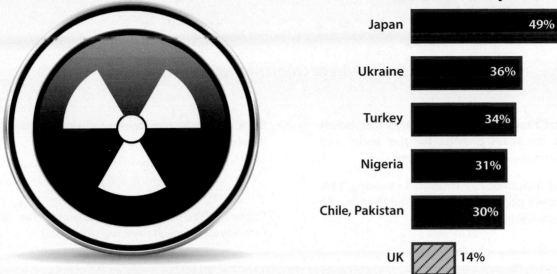

Nuclear weapons

Japan	49%
Ukraine	36%
Turkey	34%
Nigeria	31%
Chile, Pakistan	30%
UK	14%

African countries see AIDS and other infectious diseases as the most pressing issue in the world today

AIDS & other diseases

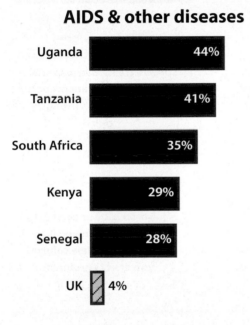

Uganda	44%
Tanzania	41%
South Africa	35%
Kenya	29%
Senegal	28%
UK	4%

AIDS & other diseases

The seven African nations say infectious disease is the top danger.

Many of these countries have high prevalence rates of HIV/AIDS and have had many disease epidemics in the last decade.

However, other problems also worry Africans - **38%** of those surveyed in Nigeria, where the terrorist Boko Haram group are based, said religious & ethnic hatred was the world's greatest threat.

Pollution & environment

Colombia	36%
Thailand	36%
Peru	35%
Philippines	34%
China	33%
UK	16%

Some issues

- In what order would you rank these threats?

- Can you explain why each region feels differently about the threats?

- What, if anything, can be done about each of these five dangers?

NB The survey was conducted before the Islamic State ("ISIS" or "ISIL") took over large areas of Iraq and Syria and posted prisoner executions online and before the Ebola outbreak in West Africa became a high-profile international story.

Source: Pew Research Center, Global Attitudes Survey 2014
www.pewresearch.org

Social progress

An index reveals where countries need to improve

The Social Progress Index measures the extent to which countries provide for the social and environmental needs of their citizens.

In 2015 it included 133 countries covering 94% of the world's population. It assessed them on 52 indicators covering:

- **Basic human needs:** Does a country provide for its people's most essential needs?
- **Wellbeing:** Are the building blocks in place for individuals and communities to improve and sustain wellbeing?
- **Opportunity:** Is there opportunity for all individuals to reach their full potential?

Social Progress Index

Basic human needs

Nutrition and basic medical care
eg undernourishment, food deficit, maternal mortality rate, stillbirth rate, child mortality rate, prevalence of tuberculosis

Air, water and sanitation
eg deaths from indoor and outdoor air pollution, access to piped water, rural/urban access to improved water source, access to improved sanitation facilities and wastewater treatment

Shelter
eg satisfaction with housing, access to electricity

Personal safety
eg homicide rate, level of violent crime, perceived criminality, political terror

Foundations of wellbeing

Access to basic knowledge
eg adult literacy rate, primary & secondary school enrolment, girls' average years in school

Access to information and communications
eg mobile phone subscriptions, internet users, fixed broadband subscriptions, press freedom index

Health and wellness
eg life expectancy, obesity, cancer death rate, deaths from cardiovascular disease, diabetes and HIV, availability of quality healthcare

Ecosystem sustainability
eg ecological footprint, CO_2 emissions per capita, energy use, water withdrawals

Opportunity

Personal rights
eg Political rights, freedom of speech, freedom of assembly/association, private property rights, women's property rights

Access to higher education
eg college/university enrolment, female college/university enrolment

Personal freedom and choice
eg basic religious freedoms, contraceptive prevalence, access to childcare, freedom over life choices

Equality and inclusion
eg tolerance for immigrants and homosexuals, women treated with respect, community safety net, equality of opportunity for ethnic minorities

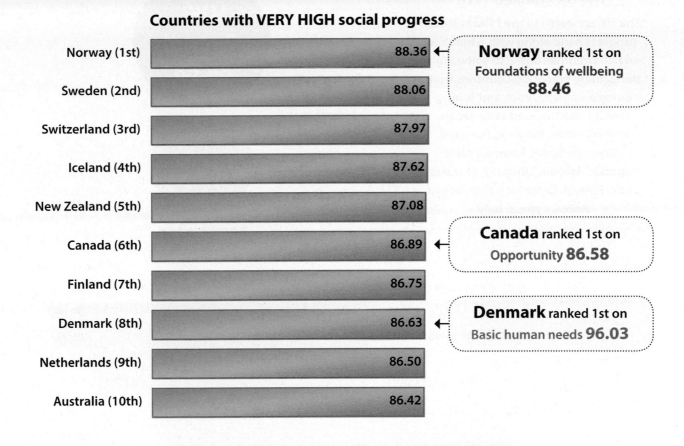

The 133 countries were given a score out of 100 and their overall ranking was broken down into 6 bands ranging from **VERY HIGH** to **VERY LOW** social progress.

Countries with VERY HIGH social progress

Norway (1st)	88.36
Sweden (2nd)	88.06
Switzerland (3rd)	87.97
Iceland (4th)	87.62
New Zealand (5th)	87.08
Canada (6th)	86.89
Finland (7th)	86.75
Denmark (8th)	86.63
Netherlands (9th)	86.50
Australia (10th)	86.42

Norway ranked 1st on **Foundations of wellbeing 88.46**

Canada ranked 1st on **Opportunity 86.58**

Denmark ranked 1st on Basic human needs **96.03**

If the world were one country, it would score **61.00** on the Social Progress Index on a population-weighted basis.

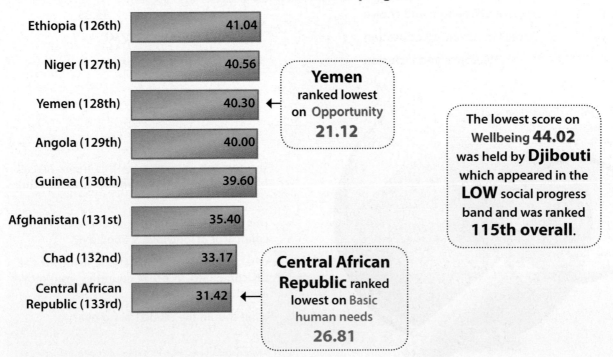

Countries with VERY LOW social progress

Ethiopia (126th)	41.04
Niger (127th)	40.56
Yemen (128th)	40.30
Angola (129th)	40.00
Guinea (130th)	39.60
Afghanistan (131st)	35.40
Chad (132nd)	33.17
Central African Republic (133rd)	31.42

Yemen ranked lowest on Opportunity **21.12**

The lowest score on Wellbeing **44.02** was held by **Djibouti** which appeared in the **LOW** social progress band and was ranked **115th overall**.

Central African Republic ranked lowest on Basic human needs **26.81**

How the UK ranked

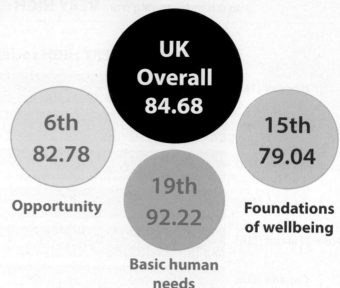

UK Overall 84.68

6th 82.78 Opportunity

19th 92.22 Basic human needs

15th 79.04 Foundations of wellbeing

Basic human needs:

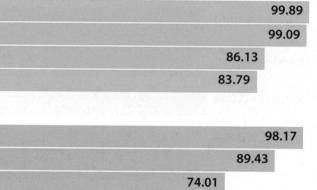

Water and sanitation	99.89
Nutrition and basic medical care	99.09
Shelter	86.13
Personal safety	83.79

Foundations of wellbeing:

Access to basic knowledge	98.17
Access to information and communications	89.43
Health and wellness	74.01
Ecosystem sustainability	54.53

Opportunity:

Personal rights	97.68
Personal freedom and choice	85.83
Access to advanced education	77.91
Tolerance and inclusion	69.68

Some issues

- The top ten countries on this index are all high-income countries. Why do you think this is?

- This index does not look at the wealth of a country or of individuals. Should it?

- What is the best thing about living in the UK compared to other countries you know about?

- What should the UK do to improve?

Source: Social Progress Index 2015 © Social Progress Imperative 2015
www.socialprogressimperative.org

Integrating immigrants

There are still many obstacles for immigrants to overcome in living, working or participating in our societies, but this is changing slowly

The Migrant Integration Policy Index (MIPEX) contrasts and compares 38 countries.

It shows that great differences exist in how these countries are integrating foreign immigrants **legally** residing there.

Scores from 167 policy indicators in 8 policy areas are averaged out and converted to percentages - 100% is the top score.

The 8 policy areas and the best and worst performing countries

Political participation

Whether non-EU migrants can vote, stand as candidates in elections and are informed about political rights.

✔ Best: Norway 82%   ✘ Worst: Romania 0%

Labour market

Whether immigrants are excluded from certain jobs and what rights they have as workers.

✔ Best: Sweden 98%   ✘ Worst: Turkey 15%

Family reunion

Whether migrants can sponsor a relative and whether the state protects a migrant's right to settle with their family.

✔ Best: Spain 90%   ✘ Worst: UK 33%

Health

Immigrants' healthcare coverage and ability to access services. Policies often fail to take their specific health needs into account.

✔ Best: New Zealand 75% ✘ Worst: Latvia 17%

Anti-discrimination

Whether religious/racial discrimination is punished and victims are encouraged to bring forward cases.

The UK has some of the strongest anti-discrimination laws and equality policies.

✔ Best: Canada 92%   ✘ Worst: Iceland 5%

Access to nationality

How long they must wait to become citizens.

✔ Best: Portugal 82%   ✘ Worst: Latvia 15%

Permanent residence

How long migrants have to wait to become permanent residents.

✔ Best: Belgium 86%   ✘ Worst: Turkey 27%

Education

How well a migrant child progresses through the education system. Migrant pupils receive better support in British schools than on the continent, and all British pupils receive the best education on living in a diverse society.

✔ Best: Sweden 77%   ✘ Worst: Bulgaria 3%

International overall comparison

Key to scores

80 - 100 Favourable	41-59 Halfway favourable	1-20 Unfavourable
60-79 Slightly favourable	21-40 Slightly unfavourable	0-19 Critically unfavourable

Top 10 countries with the MOST favourable performance within the 8 policies

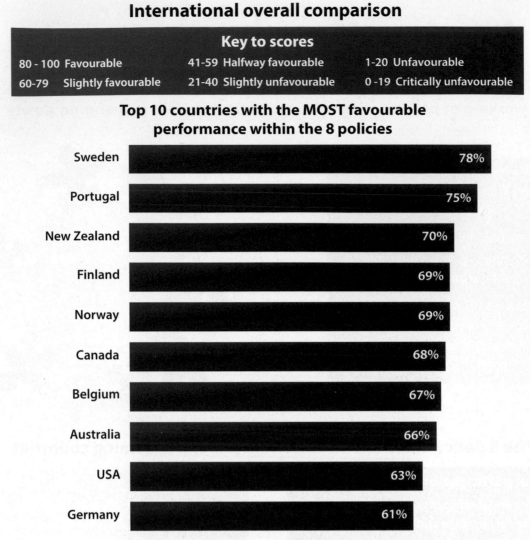

Sweden	78%
Portugal	75%
New Zealand	70%
Finland	69%
Norway	69%
Canada	68%
Belgium	67%
Australia	66%
USA	63%
Germany	61%

The 10 countries with the LEAST favourable performance within the 8 policies

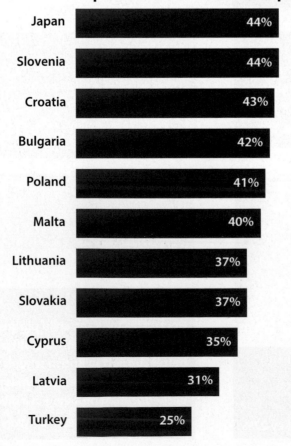

Japan	44%
Slovenia	44%
Croatia	43%
Bulgaria	42%
Poland	41%
Malta	40%
Lithuania	37%
Slovakia	37%
Cyprus	35%
Latvia	31%
Turkey	25%

The United Kingdom ranked 15th overall with a score of 57%

How the UK scored in each policy area

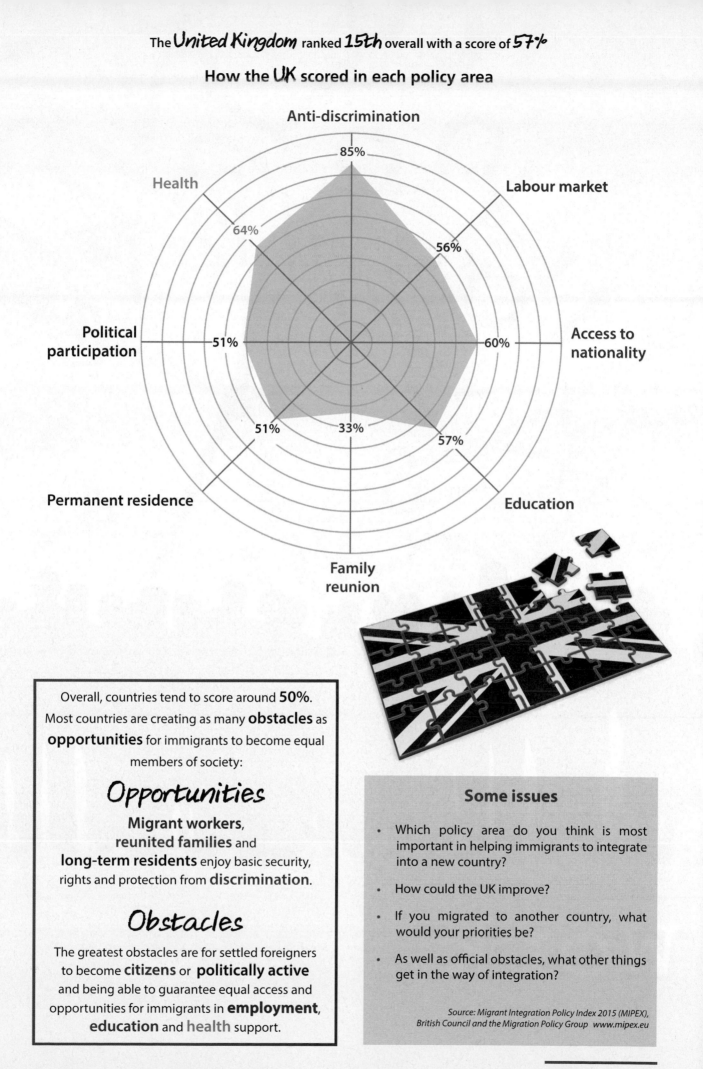

- Anti-discrimination **85%**
- Labour market **56%**
- Access to nationality **60%**
- Education **57%**
- Family reunion **33%**
- Permanent residence **51%**
- Political participation **51%**
- Health **64%**

Overall, countries tend to score around **50%**. Most countries are creating as many **obstacles** as **opportunities** for immigrants to become equal members of society:

Opportunities

Migrant workers, **reunited families** and **long-term residents** enjoy basic security, rights and protection from **discrimination**.

Obstacles

The greatest obstacles are for settled foreigners to become **citizens** or **politically active** and being able to guarantee equal access and opportunities for immigrants in **employment**, **education** and **health** support.

Some issues

- Which policy area do you think is most important in helping immigrants to integrate into a new country?

- How could the UK improve?

- If you migrated to another country, what would your priorities be?

- As well as official obstacles, what other things get in the way of integration?

Source: Migrant Integration Policy Index 2015 (MIPEX), British Council and the Migration Policy Group www.mipex.eu

Work

Making a living

The most desired jobs in Britain are not what you might expect; they are not even the most reliably well paid ones

% who say they would like to do the following jobs for a living
(Respondents were shown a random sample of 8 of the following jobs)

Job	%
Author	60%
Librarian	54%
Academic	51%
Lawyer	43%
Interior designer	41%
Journalist	39%
Doctor	39%
TV presenter	36%
Train driver	35%
Teacher	35%
Accountant	34%
Olympic athlete	31%
Member of Parliament	31%
Hollywood movie star	31%
Formula 1 driver	29%
Chef	29%
Farmer	29%
Police officer	29%
Astronaut	27%
Firefighter	26%
Investment banker	26%
Flight attendant	25%
Estate agent	23%
Model	19%
Refuse collector	16%
Taxi driver	13%
Cleaner	13%
Soldier	13%
Traffic warden	10%
Call centre worker	7%
Miner	5%

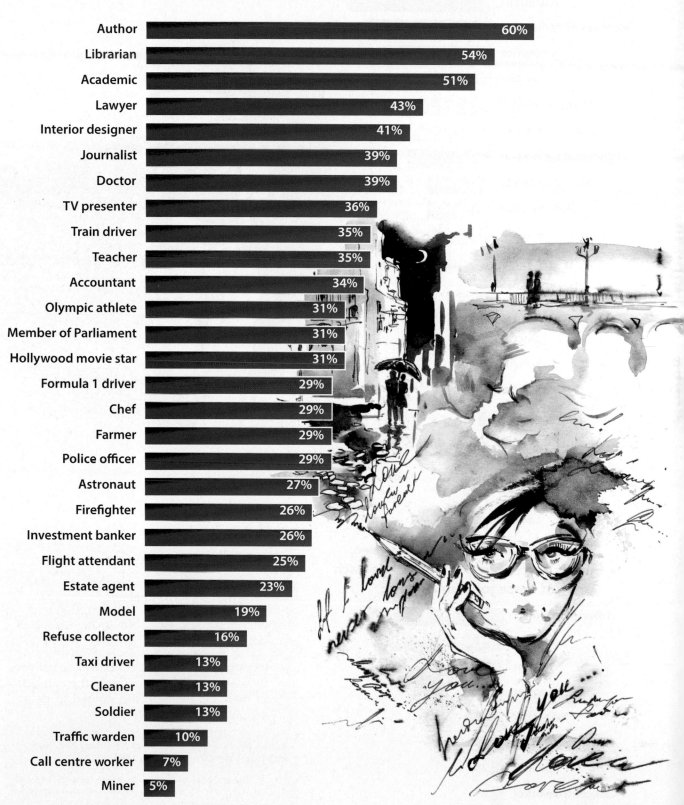

Differences in job appeal by gender

Both men and women favour the three most popular jobs of author, librarian and academic. Law, journalism, medicine and TV also feature in both of their top tens. But there are still some striking differences between genders.

Men are more likely than women, by this percentage, to want to do each of these jobs for a living:

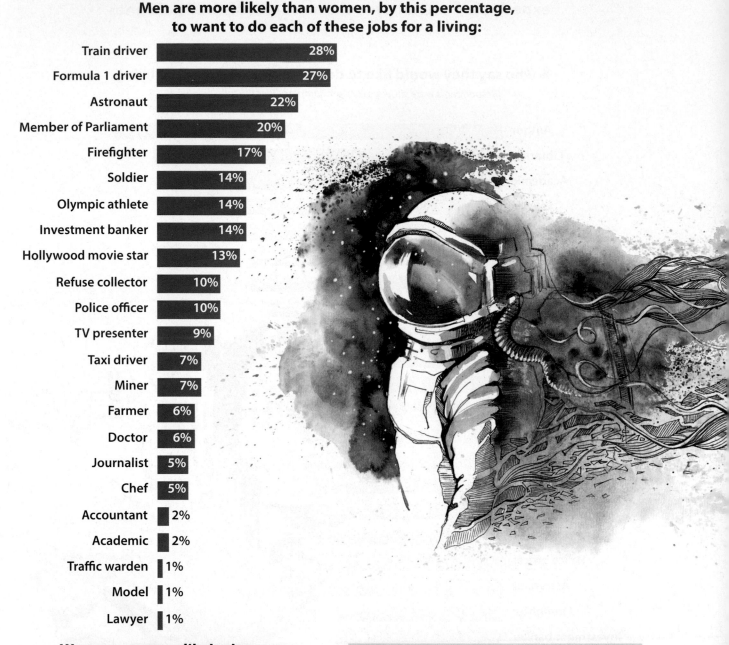

Job	Percentage
Train driver	28%
Formula 1 driver	27%
Astronaut	22%
Member of Parliament	20%
Firefighter	17%
Soldier	14%
Olympic athlete	14%
Investment banker	14%
Hollywood movie star	13%
Refuse collector	10%
Police officer	10%
TV presenter	9%
Taxi driver	7%
Miner	7%
Farmer	6%
Doctor	6%
Journalist	5%
Chef	5%
Accountant	2%
Academic	2%
Traffic warden	1%
Model	1%
Lawyer	1%

Women are more likely than men, by this percentage, to want to do each of these jobs for a living:

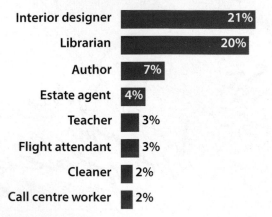

Job	Percentage
Interior designer	21%
Librarian	20%
Author	7%
Estate agent	4%
Teacher	3%
Flight attendant	3%
Cleaner	2%
Call centre worker	2%

Some issues

- What makes a job desirable?

- What job could you never imagine yourself doing, and why?

- What could be done to cut down the gender difference so that, for example, the numbers of men and women who wanted to be an astronaut were similar?

Base: A survey of 14,294 GB Adults in February 2015 (each individual base size ranging from 3,643 to 3,797).

Source: YouGov www.yougov.co.uk/news/2015/02/15/bookish-britain-academic-jobs-are-most-desired/

Occupations & earnings

Which are the highest and lowest paying jobs in Great Britain?

10 highest earning occupations
(Median gross* full-time annual earnings, April 2014, Great Britain)

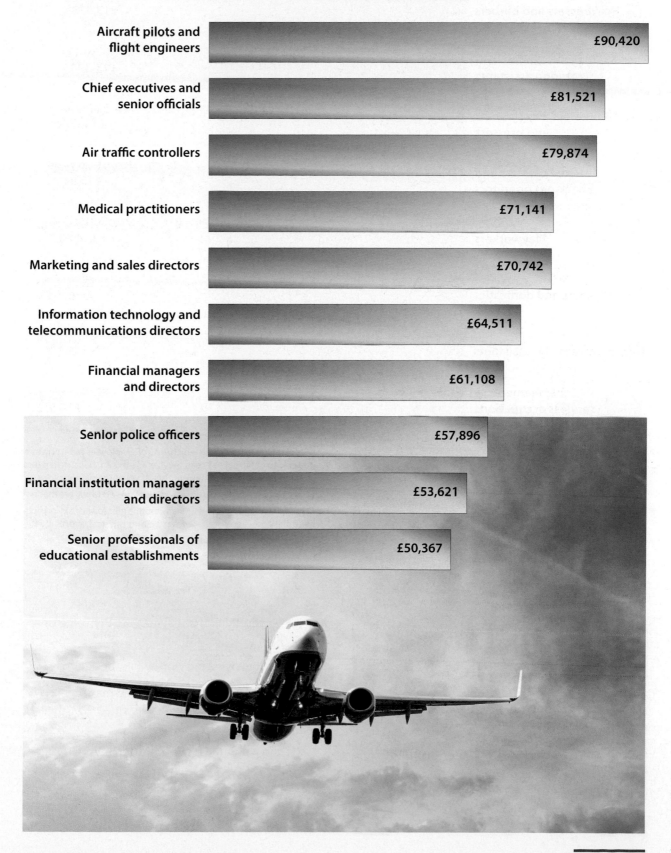

Occupation	Earnings
Aircraft pilots and flight engineers	£90,420
Chief executives and senior officials	£81,521
Air traffic controllers	£79,874
Medical practitioners	£71,141
Marketing and sales directors	£70,742
Information technology and telecommunications directors	£64,511
Financial managers and directors	£61,108
Senior police officers	£57,896
Financial institution managers and directors	£53,621
Senior professionals of educational establishments	£50,367

10 lowest earning occupations

(Median gross* full-time annual earnings, April 2014, Great Britain)

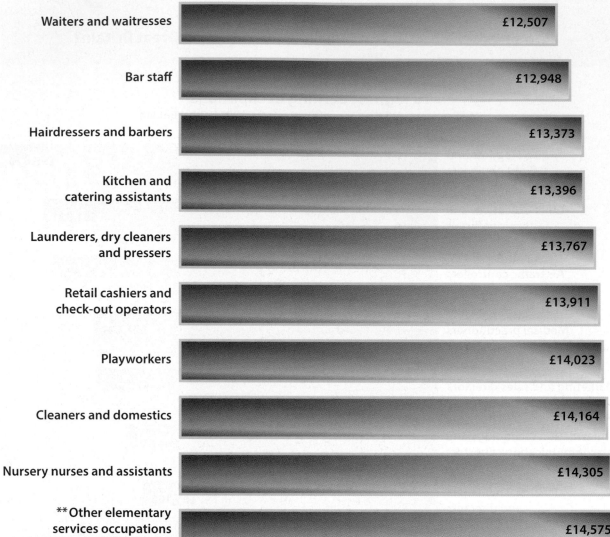

Occupation	Earnings
Waiters and waitresses	£12,507
Bar staff	£12,948
Hairdressers and barbers	£13,373
Kitchen and catering assistants	£13,396
Launderers, dry cleaners and pressers	£13,767
Retail cashiers and check-out operators	£13,911
Playworkers	£14,023
Cleaners and domestics	£14,164
Nursery nurses and assistants	£14,305
**Other elementary services occupations (not elsewhere classified)	£14,575

* Median: the value below which 50% of employees fall - it gives a better idea of typical pay than the average (mean) because it is less affected by a relatively small number of very high earners.

Gross: Employee's pay before any deductions eg taxes, are made

**Other elementary services: Mostly routine jobs (often using simple hand-held tools and sometimes requiring physical effort). Mostly not requiring formal educational qualifications.

Some issues

- Do you think that pay reflects the value of a job?

- What makes a job worthwhile, besides pay?

- Should there be minimum and maximum pay amounts?

- How should the pay rate for a job be decided and who should make the decision?

Source: Annual Survey of Hours and Earnings, Office for National Statistics © Crown copyright 2014 www.ons.gov.uk

Job satisfaction

More than a third of British workers say their job is making no meaningful contribution to the world - but most of them aren't looking for another one

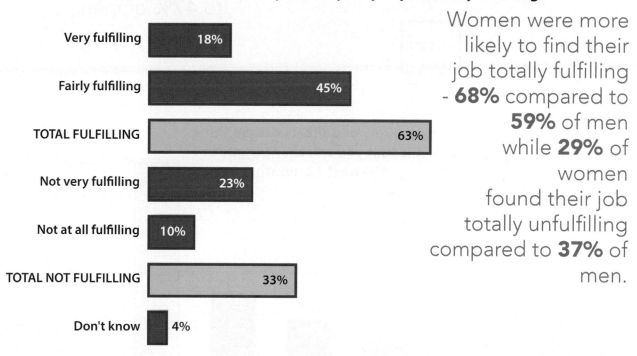

To what extent, if at all, do you find your job personally fulfilling?

- Very fulfilling — 18%
- Fairly fulfilling — 45%
- TOTAL FULFILLING — 63%
- Not very fulfilling — 23%
- Not at all fulfilling — 10%
- TOTAL NOT FULFILLING — 33%
- Don't know — 4%

Women were more likely to find their job totally fulfilling - **68%** compared to **59%** of men while **29%** of women found their job totally unfulfilling compared to **37%** of men.

Imagine you are meeting someone for the first time. Would you generally feel proud, embarrassed or neither to tell them about what you do for a living?

- Don't know (3%)
- Embarrassed (8%)
- Proud (49%)
- Neither/nor (41%)

Figures do not add up to 100% due to rounding

Do you think that your job is or is not making a meaningful contribution to the world?

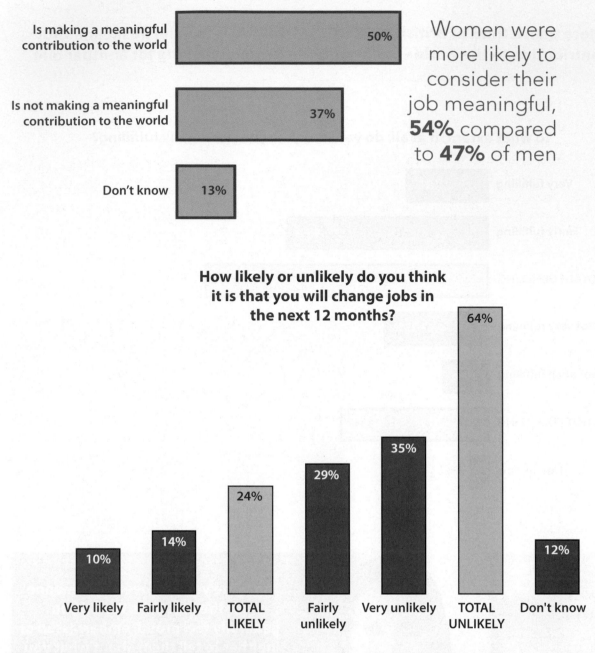

Is making a meaningful contribution to the world **50%**

Is not making a meaningful contribution to the world **37%**

Don't know **13%**

Women were more likely to consider their job meaningful, **54%** compared to **47%** of men

How likely or unlikely do you think it is that you will change jobs in the next 12 months?

Very likely	Fairly likely	TOTAL LIKELY	Fairly unlikely	Very unlikely	TOTAL UNLIKELY	Don't know
10%	14%	24%	29%	35%	64%	12%

Some issues

- What do you think makes a job feel fulfilling?

- Why do you think women find their work more fulfilling than men?

- Why do you think people who are unhappy with their work do not seek different jobs?

- Would high wages make up for doing a job you didn't enjoy?

- Would personal fulfilment be an important part of a job for you?

NB Small base - YouGov survey about workers' attitudes interviewed 849 Working GB Adults

Source: YouGov   www.yougov.co.uk

4 day week

**57% of people would prefer a 4 day working week
- as long as they don't lose out financially**

Some people say that if everyone worked a four day week instead of a five day week, we would be more productive, because we would work harder in the four days and spend more money in our time off.

Other people say that if everyone worked a four day week we would get less work done and Britain's economy would be less productive.

Do you think a four day week would be more or less economically productive than a five day week?

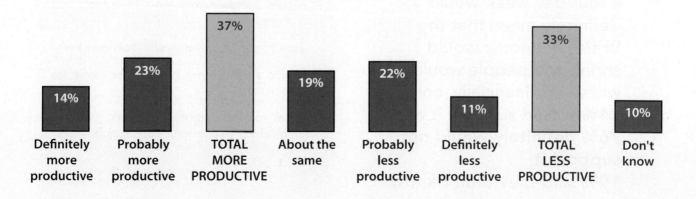

14%	23%	37%	19%	22%	11%	33%	10%
Definitely more productive	Probably more productive	TOTAL MORE PRODUCTIVE	About the same	Probably less productive	Definitely less productive	TOTAL LESS PRODUCTIVE	Don't know

Do you think as a nation we would be more or less prosperous if we worked a four day week?

More prosperous	26%
Less prosperous	32%
Would not make a difference	28%
Don't know	14%

Do you think as a nation we would be more or less happy if we worked a four day week?

Happier	71%
Would not make a difference	16%
Less happy	7%
Don't know	6%

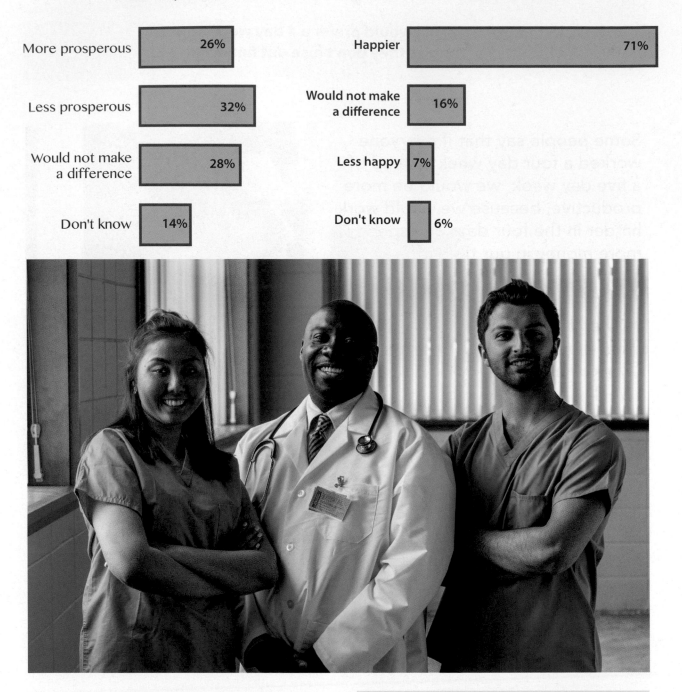

If it was demonstrated that a four day week would definitely mean that the British economy would shrink and people would be worse off financially, only **14% would support** it while **76% definitely would not support it.**
10% said they **didn't know.**

Some issues

- Would a 4 day week work in schools and colleges?

- How might a 4 day week affect people's lives?

- Would a 4 day week be better or worse for businesses?

- What other changes to work patterns might help people enjoy their work more?

In September 2014 YouGov interviewed 2,162 adults about working a 4 day week

Source: YouGov www.yougov.co.uk

Young people

Abusive relationships

Many young people have experienced violence at the hands of a partner

A survey explored four different types of interpersonal violence and abuse - each type of violence was measured by a range of questions.

Face-to-face emotional violence

Have any of your partners ever done any of these things face-to-face:

- Put you down in a nasty way?
- Shouted at you/screamed in your face/called you names?
- Said negative things about your appearance, body, friends or family?
- Threatened to hurt you physically?

Percentage of young people who said these things had happened to them:

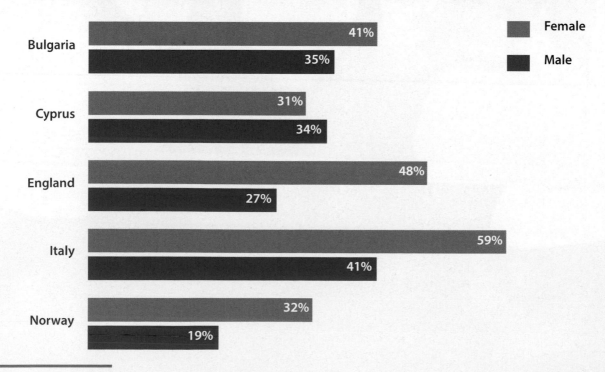

	Female	Male
Bulgaria	41%	35%
Cyprus	31%	34%
England	48%	27%
Italy	59%	41%
Norway	32%	19%

Online emotional violence

Have any of your partners ever done any of these things using a mobile phone, computer or tablet:

- Put you down or ever sent you any nasty messages?

- Posted nasty messages about you that others could see?

- Sent you threatening messages?

- Tried to control who you could be friends with or where you could go?

- Constantly checked up on what you had been doing/who you had seen, eg by sending you messages or checking your social networking page all the time?

- Used mobile phones or social networking sites to stop your friends liking you, eg pretending to be you and sending nasty messages to your friends?

Percentage of young people who said these things had happened to them

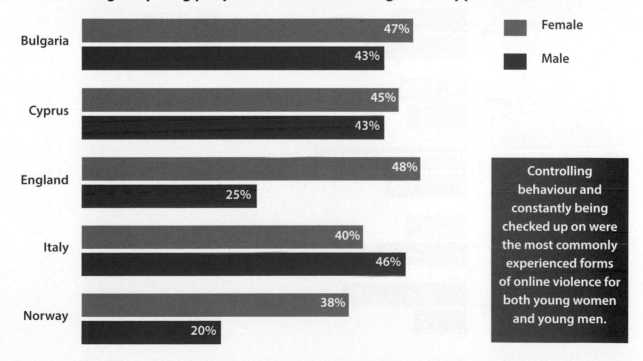

Country	Female	Male
Bulgaria	47%	43%
Cyprus	45%	43%
England	48%	25%
Italy	40%	46%
Norway	38%	20%

Controlling behaviour and constantly being checked up on were the most commonly experienced forms of online violence for both young women and young men.

Physical violence

Have any of your partners ever done any of these things:

- Used physical force such as slapping, pushing, hitting or holding you down?

- Used more severe physical force such as punching, strangling, beating you up, hitting you with an object?

Percentage of young people who said these things had happened to them:

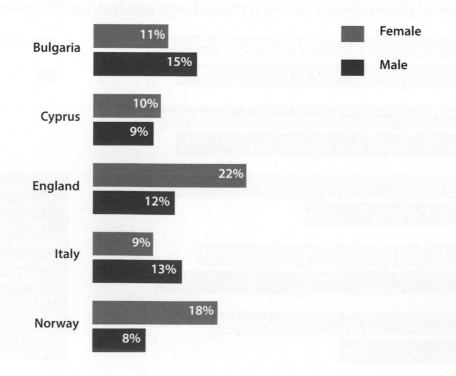

	Female	Male
Bulgaria	11%	15%
Cyprus	10%	9%
England	22%	12%
Italy	9%	13%
Norway	18%	8%

Sexual violence

Have any of your partners ever done any of these things:

- Pressured you into intimate touching or something else?

- Physically forced you into intimate touching or something else?

- Pressured you into having sexual intercourse?

- Physically forced you into having sexual intercourse?

Percentage of young people who said these things had happened to them:

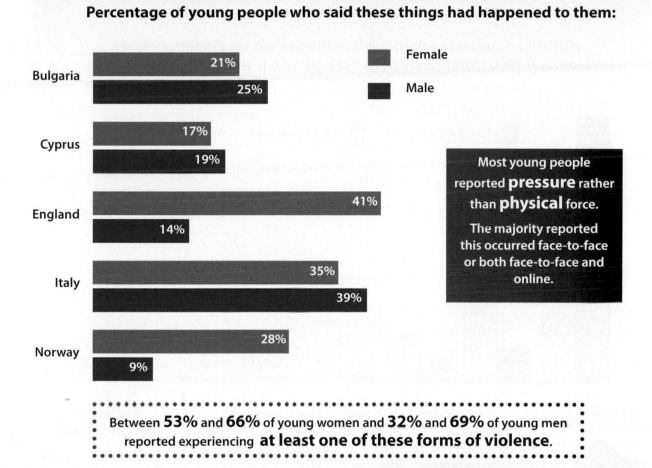

Female

Male

Bulgaria 21% / 25%

Cyprus 17% / 19%

England 41% / 14%

Italy 35% / 39%

Norway 28% / 9%

Most young people reported **pressure** rather than **physical** force.

The majority reported this occurred face-to-face or both face-to-face and online.

Between **53%** and **66%** of young women and **32%** and **69%** of young men reported experiencing **at least one of these forms of violence**.

Helpful organisations

This is Abuse http://thisisabuse.direct.gov.uk

ChildLine Tel: 0800 1111 www.childline.org.uk

Campaign Against Domestic Violence
24 hour Freephone: 0808 2000 247

The Respect freephone: 0808 802 4040
respectphoneline.org.uk

The Men's freephone Advice Line:
0808 801 0327 mensadviceline.org.uk

The Site www.thesite.org/sex-and-relationships/relationships/women-and-domestic-violence-9161.html

NSPCC www.nspcc.org.uk/preventing-abuse/child-abuse-and-neglect/domestic-abuse/

Some issues

- Online emotional violence is the most common form across the different countries. Why do you think this is?

- In almost all cases, girls in England were most likely to have experienced violence. Why might that be?

- Why do you think there is a wide variation in the responses from the different countries?

- What can be done to prevent each of these forms of abuse?

Base: A school survey of 3,277 young people across five European countries: Bulgaria, Cyprus, England, Italy and Norway. Respondents were aged between 14 and 17 years-old, and had been in a relationship.

Source: Safeguarding Teenage Intimate Relationships (STIR)
http://stiritup.eu/young-people

Sexuality

Young people have an open-minded approach to their own sexuality

The Kinsey* scale plots individuals on a range of sexual dispositions from exclusively heterosexual at 0 through to exclusively homosexual at 6. YouGov simply asked people to place themselves on the sexuality scale.

British adults were asked to place themselves on the Kinsey scale, ranging from 0 (completely heterosexual) to 6 (completely homosexual)

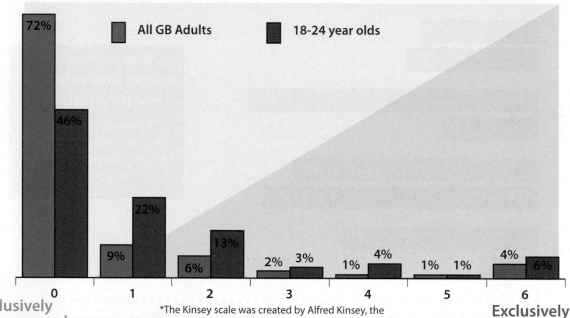

Legend: All GB Adults | 18-24 year olds

	0	1	2	3	4	5	6
All GB Adults	72%	9%	6%	2%	1%	1%	4%
18-24 year olds	46%	22%	13%	3%	4%	1%	6%

Exclusively heterosexual (0)   **Exclusively homosexual** (6)

*The Kinsey scale was created by Alfred Kinsey, the eminent researcher into human sexuality, in the 1940s.

A total of **1%** identified as asexual (without any sexual feelings), **3%** were unsure of their orientation and the remaining **1%** reflected the rounding up of the figures in each category to create whole numbers.

These figures are not measures of active bisexuality - overall, 89% of the population describes themselves as heterosexual - but putting yourself at level 1 allows for the possibility of homosexual feelings and experiences.

When YouGov asked 1,632 British adults to rank their sexuality on the Kinsey scale, a clear difference emerged - the younger the age group, the less likely a person is to see their sexuality as fixed in stone.

In the younger age group there is little difference between those who have a flexible view of their sexuality (43%) and those who consider their sexuality as fixed, either completely heterosexual or completely homosexual (52%). In the oldest age group the difference is much greater.

British adults were asked to place themselves on the Kinsey scale, ranging from 0 (completely heterosexual) to 6 (completely homosexual), age breakdown

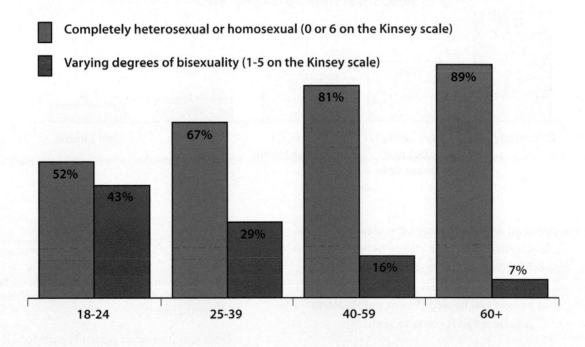

■ Completely heterosexual or homosexual (0 or 6 on the Kinsey scale)

■ Varying degrees of bisexuality (1-5 on the Kinsey scale)

Age	Completely hetero/homosexual	Varying degrees of bisexuality
18-24	52%	43%
25-39	67%	29%
40-59	81%	16%
60+	89%	7%

Of the 52% of 18-24 year-olds who place themselves entirely at one end of the scale or the other, 46% say they are completely heterosexual and 6% say they are completely homosexual.

Thinking about sexuality, which of the following comes closer to your view?

Responses from 18-24 year olds

Don't know (8%)

There is no middle ground, you are either heterosexual or homosexual (18%)

Sexuality is a scale – it is possible to be somewhere near the middle (74%)

Those who identified as heterosexual were asked:
"If the right person came along at the right time, do you think it is conceivable that you could be attracted to a person of the same sex?"

Responses from 18-24 year olds

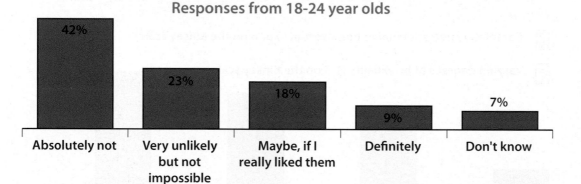

Absolutely not	Very unlikely but not impossible	Maybe, if I really liked them	Definitely	Don't know
42%	23%	18%	9%	7%

People of all ages now accept the idea that sexual orientation is not just a choice between two opposites. Overall **60%** of heterosexuals and **73%** of homosexuals support the idea that people can be at different points along a scale when it come to sexuality.

However, there is a noticeable difference across age groups.

32% of those aged 60+ felt there was no middle ground in terms of sexuality.

68% of the 60+ age group replied 'Absolutely not' when asked if they could ever be attracted to someone of the same sex.

Some issues

- Do you think that people are more open minded about sexuality today than in earlier generations?

- Does it matter what sexuality a person is?

- Do you think attitudes will continue to change about sexuality?

- Why are these findings important?

Source: YouGov www.yougov.co.uk

Young drinkers

The drinking behaviour of young adults has changed

Young people are drinking less than ever before

Proportion of young people (16-24) who...

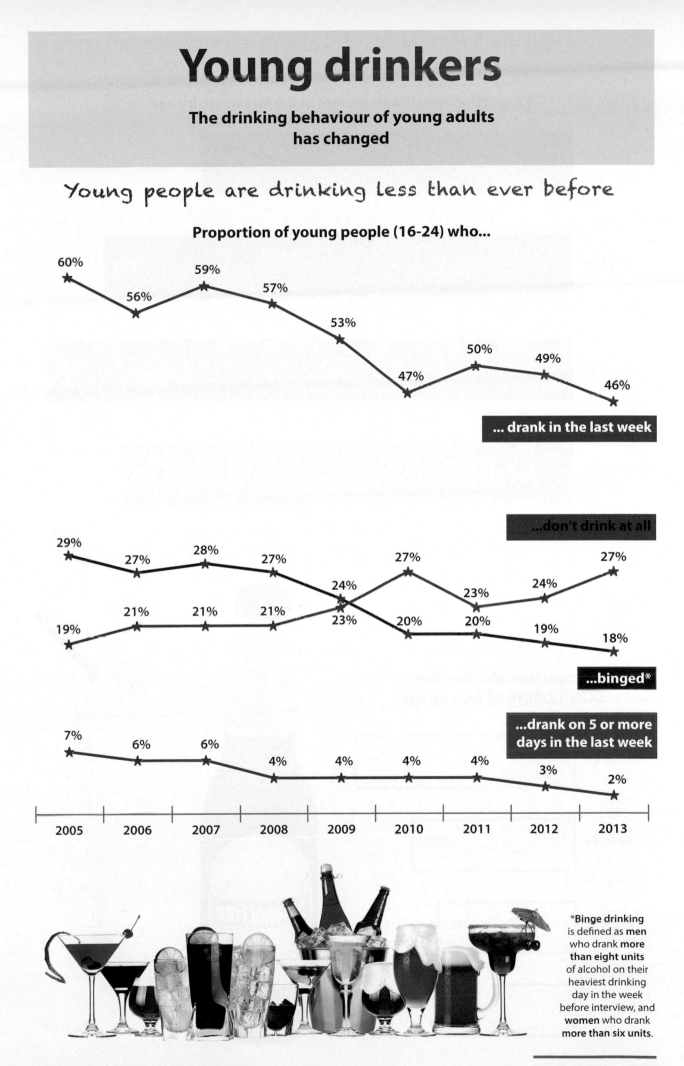

... drank in the last week

60%
56%
59%
57%
53%
47%
50%
49%
46%

...don't drink at all

29%
27%
28%
27%
24%
27%
23%
24%
27%

19%
21%
21%
21%
23%
20%
20%
19%
18%

...binged*

...drank on 5 or more days in the last week

7%
6%
6%
4%
4%
4%
4%
3%
2%

2005   2006   2007   2008   2009   2010   2011   2012   2013

*Binge drinking is defined as **men** who drank **more than eight units** of alcohol on their heaviest drinking day in the week before interview, and **women** who drank **more than six units**.

How young people's drinking compares to other age groups, Great Britain 2013

Proportion who drank alcohol in the last week, by age

Age	%
16 to 24	46%
25 to 44	58%
45 to 64	65%
65 and over	56%

Teetotallers

Proportion who say they DON'T DRINK AT ALL, by age

Age	%
16 to 24	27%
25 to 44	20%
45 to 64	17%
65 and over	27%

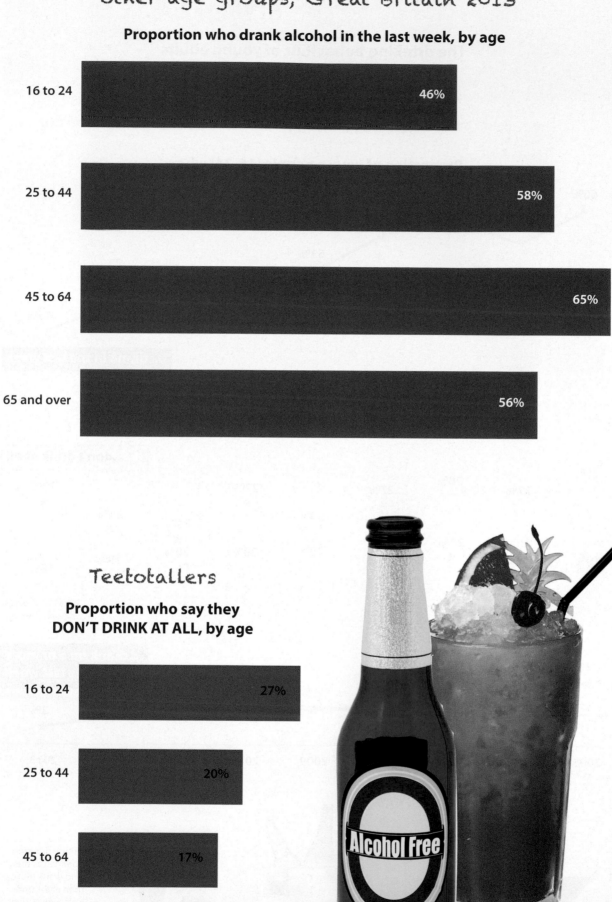

Proportion binge drinking, by age

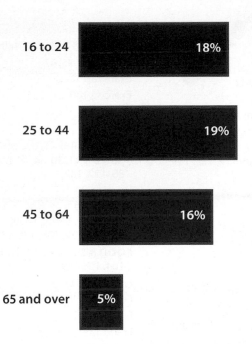

16 to 24	18%
25 to 44	19%
45 to 64	16%
65 and over	5%

Frequent drinkers

Proportion who drank alcohol on five on more days in the last week

16 to 24	2%
25 to 44	6%
45 to 64	14%
65 and over	18%

Some issues

- In your opinion, what could influence the amount someone drinks?

- Are you surprised by any of the figures for the different age groups?

- Would you expect the downward trend in young people's drinking to continue?

- Is it possible to drink alcohol regularly without any effects on your health?

Source: Adult Drinking Habits in Great Britain 2013
© Office for National Statistics 2015   www.ons.gov.uk

Entries in **colour** refer to main sections. Page numbers refer to the first page. Most charts contain UK or GB information.

Complete Issues

understanding our world